Mastering Predictive Analytics with scikit-learn and TensorFlow

Implement machine learning techniques to build advanced predictive models using Python

Alan Fontaine

BIRMINGHAM - MUMBAI

Mastering Predictive Analytics with scikit-learn and TensorFlow

Commissioning Editor: Sunith Shetty
Acquisition Editor: Namrata Patil
Content Development Editor: Athikho Sapuni Rishana
Technical Editor: Joseph Sunil
Copy Editor: Safis Editing
Project Coordinator: Kirti Pisat
Proofreader: Safis Editing
Indexer: Rekha Nair
Graphics: Jisha Chirayil
Production Coordinator: Deepika Naik

First published: September 2018

Production reference: 1280918

Published by Packt Publishing Ltd.
Livery Place
35 Livery Street
Birmingham
B3 2PB, UK.

ISBN 978-1-78961-774-0

www.packtpub.com

`mapt.io`

Mapt is an online digital library that gives you full access to over 5,000 books and videos, as well as industry leading tools to help you plan your personal development and advance your career. For more information, please visit our website.

Why subscribe?

- Spend less time learning and more time coding with practical eBooks and Videos from over 4,000 industry professionals

- Improve your learning with Skill Plans built especially for you

- Get a free eBook or video every month

- Mapt is fully searchable

- Copy and paste, print, and bookmark content

Packt.com

Did you know that Packt offers eBook versions of every book published, with PDF and ePub files available? You can upgrade to the eBook version at `www.packt.com` and as a print book customer, you are entitled to a discount on the eBook copy. Get in touch with us at `customercare@packtpub.com` for more details.

At `www.packt.com`, you can also read a collection of free technical articles, sign up for a range of free newsletters, and receive exclusive discounts and offers on Packt books and eBooks.

Contributor

About the author

Alan Fontaine is a data scientist with more than 12 years of experience in analytical roles. He has been a consultant for many projects in fields such as: business, education, medicine, mass media, among others. He is a big Python fan and has been using it routinely for five years for analyzing data, building models, producing reports, making predictions, and building interactive applications that transform data into intelligence.

Packt is searching for authors like you

If you're interested in becoming an author for Packt, please visit authors.packtpub.com and apply today. We have worked with thousands of developers and tech professionals, just like you, to help them share their insight with the global tech community. You can make a general application, apply for a specific hot topic that we are recruiting an author for, or submit your own idea.

Table of Contents

Preface   1

Chapter 1: Ensemble Methods for Regression and Classification   7
  Ensemble methods and their working   8
    Bootstrap sampling   9
    Bagging   10
    Random forests   11
    Boosting   11
  Ensemble methods for regression   11
    The diamond dataset   12
    Training different regression models   15
      KNN model   15
      Bagging model   16
      Random forests model   16
      Boosting model   17
  Using ensemble methods for classification   20
    Predicting a credit card dataset   20
    Training different regression models   24
      Logistic regression model   24
      Bagging model   25
      Random forest model   26
      Boosting model   27
  Summary   33

Chapter 2: Cross-validation and Parameter Tuning   35
  Holdout cross-validation   36
  K-fold cross-validation   36
    Implementing k-fold cross-validation   38
  Comparing models with k-fold cross-validation   41
  Introduction to hyperparameter tuning   45
    Exhaustive grid search   46
    Hyperparameter tuning in scikit-learn   46
    Comparing tuned and untuned models   51
  Summary   52

Chapter 3: Working with Features   53
  Feature selection methods   53
    Removing dummy features with low variance   54
    Identifying important features statistically   55
    Recursive feature elimination   55
  Dimensionality reduction and PCA   65

Feature engineering 72
    Creating new features 72
Improving models with feature engineering 80
    Training your model 84
Reducible and irreducible error 87
Summary 88

Chapter 4: Introduction to Artificial Neural Networks and TensorFlow 89
Introduction to ANNs 90
    Perceptrons 90
    Multilayer perceptron 93
Elements of a deep neural network model 96
    Deep learning 96
    Elements of an MLP model 97
Introduction to TensorFlow 100
    TensorFlow installation 100
Core concepts in TensorFlow 103
    Tensors 104
    Computational graph 104
Summary 110

Chapter 5: Predictive Analytics with TensorFlow and Deep Neural Networks 111
Predictions with TensorFlow 111
    Introduction to the MNIST dataset 112
    Building classification models using MNIST dataset 113
    Elements of the DNN model 113
    Building the DNN 115
        Reading the data 115
        Defining the architecture 115
        Placeholders for inputs and labels 116
        Building the neural network 116
        The loss function 117
        Defining optimizer and training operations 117
        Training strategy and valuation of accuracy of the classification 118
        Running the computational graph 119
Regression with Deep Neural Networks (DNN) 121
    Elements of the DNN model 122
    Building the DNN 122
        Reading the data 123
        Objects for modeling 123
        Training strategy 123
        Input pipeline for the DNN 124
        Defining the architecture 124
        Placeholders for input values and labels 124
        Building the DNN 125
        The loss function 125

      Defining optimizer and training operations   125
      Running the computational graph   126

Classification with DNNs   129
   Exponential linear unit activation function   130
   Classification with DNNs   131
   Elements of the DNN model   131
   Building the DNN   132
      Reading the data   132
      Producing the objects for modeling   133
      Training strategy   133
      Input pipeline for DNN   133
      Defining the architecture   134
      Placeholders for inputs and labels   134
      Building the neural network   134
      The loss function   135
      Evaluation nodes   135
      Optimizer and the training operation   135
      Run the computational graph   136
   Evaluating the model with a set threshold   137
  Summary   137

Appendix A: Other Books You May Enjoy   139
  Leave a review - let other readers know what you think   141

Index   143

Preface

Python is a programming language that provides various features in the field of data science. In this book, we will be touching upon two Python libraries, scikit-learn and TensorFlow. We will learn about the various implementations of ensemble methods, how they are used with real-world datasets, and how they improve prediction accuracy in classification and regression problems.

This book starts with studying ensemble methods and their features. We will look at how scikit-learn provides the right tools to choose hyperparameters for models. From there, we will get down to the nitty-gritty of predictive analytics and explore its various features and characteristics. We will be introduced to artificial neural networks, TensorFlow, and the core concepts used to build neural networks.

In the final section, we will consider factors such as computational power, improved methods, and software enhancements for efficient predictive analytics. You will become well versed in using DNNs to solve common challenges.

Who this book is for

This book is for data analysts, software engineers, and machine learning developers who are interested in implementing advanced predictive analytics using Python. Business intelligence experts will also find this book indispensable as it will teach them how to go from basic predictive models to building advanced models and producing better predictions. Knowledge of Python and familiarity with predictive analytics concepts are assumed.

What this book covers

Chapter 1, *Ensemble Methods for Regression and Classification*, covers the application of ensemble methods or algorithms to produce accurate predictions of models. We will go through the application of ensemble methods for regression and classification problems.

Chapter 2, *Cross-validation and Parameter Tuning*, explores various techniques to combine and build better models. We will learn different methods of cross-validation, including holdout cross-validation and k-fold cross-validation. We will also discuss what hyperparameter tuning is.

Chapter 3, *Working with Features*, explores feature selection methods, dimensionality reduction, PCA, and feature engineering. We will also study methods to improve models with feature engineering.

Chapter 4, *Introduction to Artificial Neural Networks and TensorFlow*, is an introduction to ANNs and TensorFlow. We will explore the various elements in the network and their functions. We will also learn the basic concepts of TensorFlow in it.

Chapter 5, *Predictive Analytics with TensorFlow and Deep Neural Networks*, explores predictive analytics with the help of TensorFlow and deep learning. We will study the MNIST dataset and classification of models using this dataset. We will learn about DNNs, their functions, and the application of DNNs to the MNIST dataset.

To get the most out of this book

This book presents some of the most advanced predictive analytics tools, models, and techniques. The main goal is to show the viewer how to improve the performance of predictive models, firstly, by showing how to build more complex models, and secondly by showing how to use related techniques that dramatically improve the quality of predictive models.

Download the example code files

You can download the example code files for this book from your account at www.packt.com. If you purchased this book elsewhere, you can visit www.packt.com/support and register to have the files emailed directly to you.

You can download the code files by following these steps:

1. Log in or register at www.packt.com.
2. Select the **SUPPORT** tab.
3. Click on **Code Downloads & Errata**.
4. Enter the name of the book in the **Search** box and follow the onscreen instructions.

Once the file is downloaded, please make sure that you unzip or extract the folder using the latest version of:

- WinRAR/7-Zip for Windows
- Zipeg/iZip/UnRarX for Mac
- 7-Zip/PeaZip for Linux

The code bundle for the book is also hosted on GitHub at `https://github.com/PacktPublishing/Mastering-Predictive-Analytics-with-scikit-learn-and-TensorFlow`. In case there's an update to the code, it will be updated on the existing GitHub repository.

We also have other code bundles from our rich catalog of books and videos available at `https://github.com/PacktPublishing/`. Check them out!

Download the color images

We also provide a PDF file that has color images of the screenshots/diagrams used in this book. You can download it here: `http://www.packtpub.com/sites/default/files/downloads/9781789617740_ColorImages.pdf`.

Conventions used

There are a number of text conventions used throughout this book.

`CodeInText`: Indicates code words in text, database table names, folder names, filenames, file extensions, pathnames, dummy URLs, user input, and Twitter handles. Here is an example: "The following screenshot shows the lines of code used for importing the `train_test_split` function and the `RobustScaler` method."

A block of code is set as follows:

```
import numpy as np
import matplotlib.pyplot as plt
import pandas as pd
%matplotlib inline
```

Bold: Indicates a new term, an important word, or words that you see onscreen. For example, words in menus or dialog boxes appear in the text like this. Here is an example: "The method used to choose the best estimators for a particular dataset or choosing the best values for all hyperparameters is called **hyperparameter tuning**."

 Warnings or important notes appear like this.

 Tips and tricks appear like this.

Get in touch

Feedback from our readers is always welcome.

General feedback: If you have questions about any aspect of this book, mention the book title in the subject of your message and email us at customercare@packtpub.com.

Errata: Although we have taken every care to ensure the accuracy of our content, mistakes do happen. If you have found a mistake in this book, we would be grateful if you would report this to us. Please visit www.packt.com/submit-errata, selecting your book, clicking on the Errata Submission Form link, and entering the details.

Piracy: If you come across any illegal copies of our works in any form on the Internet, we would be grateful if you would provide us with the location address or website name. Please contact us at copyright@packt.com with a link to the material.

If you are interested in becoming an author: If there is a topic that you have expertise in and you are interested in either writing or contributing to a book, please visit authors.packtpub.com.

Reviews

Please leave a review. Once you have read and used this book, why not leave a review on the site that you purchased it from? Potential readers can then see and use your unbiased opinion to make purchase decisions, we at Packt can understand what you think about our products, and our authors can see your feedback on their book. Thank you!

For more information about Packt, please visit `packt.com`.

1
Ensemble Methods for Regression and Classification

Advanced analytical tools are widely used by business enterprises in order to solve problems using data. The goal of analytical tools is to analyze data and extract relevant information that can be used to solve problems or increase performance of some aspect of the business. It also involves various machine learning algorithms with which we can create predictive models for better results.

In this chapter, we are going to explore a simple idea that can drastically improve the performance of basic predictive models.

We are going to cover the following topics in this chapter:

- Ensemble methods and their working
- Ensemble methods for regression
- Ensemble methods for classification

Ensemble methods and their working

Ensemble methods are based on a very simple idea: instead of using a single model to make a prediction, we use many models and then use some method to **aggregate** the predictions. Having different models is like having different points of view, and it has been demonstrated that by aggregating models that offer a different point of view; predictions can be more accurate. These methods further improve generalization over a single model because they reduce the risk of selecting a poorly performing classifier:

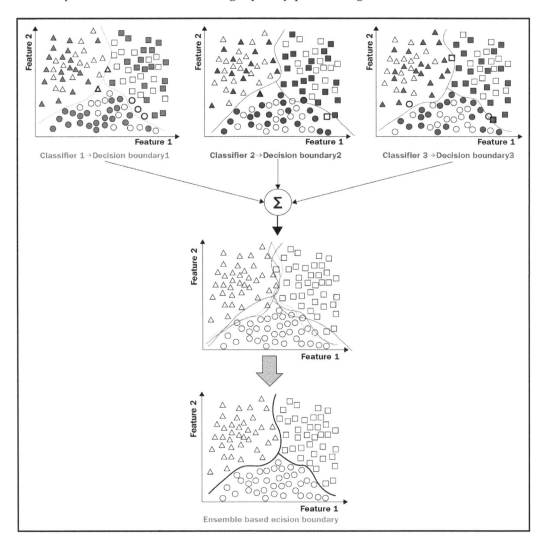

In the preceding diagram, we can see that each object belongs to one of three classes: triangles, circles, and squares. In this simplified example, we have two features to separate or classify the objects into the different classes. As you can see here, we can use three different classifiers and all the three classifiers represent different approaches and have different kinds of decision boundaries.

Ensemble learning combines all those individual predictions into a single one. The predictions made from combining the three boundaries usually have better properties than the ones produced by the individual models. This is the simple idea behind ensemble methods, also called **ensemble learning**.

The most commonly used ensemble methods are as follows:

- Bootstrap sampling
- Bagging
- Random forests
- Boosting

Before giving a high-level explanation of these methods, we need to discuss a very important statistical technique known as **bootstrap sampling**.

Bootstrap sampling

Many ensemble learning methods use a statistical technique called bootstrap sampling. A bootstrap sample of a dataset is another dataset that's obtained by randomly sampling the observations from the original dataset *with replacement*.

This technique is heavily used in statistics, for example; it is used for estimating standard errors on sample statistics like mean or standard deviation of values.

Let's understand this technique more by taking a look at the following diagram:

Let's assume that we have a population of 1 to 10, which can be considered original population data. To get a bootstrap sample, we need to draw 10 samples from the original data with replacement. Imagine you have the 10 numbers written in 10 cards in a hat; for the first element of your sample, you take one card at random from the hat and write it down, then put the card back in the hat and this process goes on until you get 10 elements. This is your bootstrap sample. As you can see in the preceding example, **9** is repeated thrice in the bootstrap sample.

This resampling of numbers with replacement improves the accuracy of the true population data. It also helps in understanding various discrepancies and features involved in the resampling process, thereby increasing accuracy of the same.

Bagging

Bagging, also known as bootstrap aggregation, is a general purpose procedure for reducing variance in the machine learning model. It is based on the bootstrap sampling technique and is generally used with regression or classification trees, but in principle this bagging technique can be used with any model.

The following steps are involved in the bagging process:

1. We choose the number of estimators or individual models to use. Let's consider this as parameter B.
2. We take sample datasets from B with replacement using the bootstrap sampling from the training set.
3. For every one of these training datasets, we fit the machine learning model in each of the bootstrap samples. This way, we get individual predictors for the B parameter.
4. We get the ensemble prediction by aggregating all of the individual predictions.

In the regression problem, the most common way to get the ensemble prediction would be to find the average of all of the individual predictions.

In the classification problem, the most common way to get the aggregated predictions is by doing a majority vote. The majority vote can be explained by an example. Let's say that we have 100 individual predictors and 80 of them vote for one particular category. Then, we choose that category as our aggregated prediction. This is what a majority vote means.

Random forests

This ensemble method is specifically created for regression or classification trees. It is very similar to bagging since, here, each individual tree is trained on a bootstrap sample of the training dataset. The difference with bagging is that it makes the model very powerful, and on splitting a node from the tree, the split that is picked is the best among a random subset of the features. So, every individual predictor considers a random subset of the features. This has the effect of making each individual predictor slightly worse and more biased but, due to the correlation of the individual predictors, the overall ensemble is generally better than the individual predictors.

Boosting

Boosting is another approach to ensemble learning. There are many methods for boosting, but one of the most successful and popular methods that people use for ensemble learning has been the **AdaBoost** algorithm. It is also called **adaptive boosting**. The core idea behind this algorithm is that, instead of fitting many individual predictors individually, we fit a sequence of weak learners. The next algorithm depends on the result of the previous one. In the AdaBoost algorithm, every iteration reweights all of these samples. The training data here reweights based on the result of the previous individual learners or individual models.

For example, in classification, the basic idea is that the examples that are misclassified gain weight and the examples that are classified correctly lose weight. So, the next learner in the sequence or the next model in the sequence focuses more on misclassified examples.

Ensemble methods for regression

Regarding regression, we will train these different models and later compare their results. In order to test all of these models, we will need a sample dataset. We are going to use this in order to implement these methods on the given dataset and see how this helps us with the performance of our models.

The diamond dataset

Let's make actual predictions about diamond prices by using different ensemble learning models. We will use a diamonds dataset(which can be found here: `https://www.kaggle.com/shivam2503/diamonds`). This dataset has the prices, among other features, of almost 54,000 diamonds. The following are the features that we have in this dataset:

- **Feature information**: A dataframe with 53,940 rows and 10 variables
- **Price**: Price in US dollars

The following are the nine predictive features:

- `carat`: This feature represents weight of the diamond (0.2-5.01)
- `cut`: This feature represents quality of the cut (`Fair`, `Good`, `Very Good`, `Premium`, and `Ideal`)
- `color`: This feature represents diamond color, from `J` (worst) to `D` (best)
- `clarity`: This feature represents a measurement of how clear the diamond is (`I1` (worst), `SI2`, `SI1`, `VS2`, `VS1`, `VVS2`, `VVS1`, `IF` (best))
- `x`: This feature represents length of diamond in mm (0-10.74)
- `y`: This feature represents width of diamond in mm (0-58.9)
- `z`: This feature represents depth of diamond in mm (0-31.8)
- `depth`: This feature represents $z/\text{mean}(x, y) = 2 * z/(x + y)$ (43-79)
- `table`: This feature represents width of the top of the diamond relative to the widest point (43-95)

The `x`, `y`, and `z` variables denote the size of the diamonds.

The libraries that we will use are `numpy`, `matplotlib`, and `pandas`. For importing these libraries, the following lines of code can be used:

```
import numpy as np
import matplotlib.pyplot as plt
import pandas as pd
%matplotlib inline
```

The following screenshot shows the lines of code that we use to call the raw dataset:

```
In [2]:  # importing data
         data_path= '../data/diamonds.csv'
         diamonds = pd.read_csv(data_path)
         diamonds.head(10)
```

Out[2]:

	carat	cut	color	clarity	depth	table	price	x	y	z
0	0.23	Ideal	E	SI2	61.5	55.0	326	3.95	3.98	2.43
1	0.21	Premium	E	SI1	59.8	61.0	326	3.89	3.84	2.31
2	0.23	Good	E	VS1	56.9	65.0	327	4.05	4.07	2.31
3	0.29	Premium	I	VS2	62.4	58.0	334	4.20	4.23	2.63
4	0.31	Good	J	SI2	63.3	58.0	335	4.34	4.35	2.75
5	0.24	Very Good	J	VVS2	62.8	57.0	336	3.94	3.96	2.48
6	0.24	Very Good	I	VVS1	62.3	57.0	336	3.95	3.98	2.47
7	0.26	Very Good	H	SI1	61.9	55.0	337	4.07	4.11	2.53
8	0.22	Fair	E	VS2	65.1	61.0	337	3.87	3.78	2.49
9	0.23	Very Good	H	VS1	59.4	61.0	338	4.00	4.05	2.39

The preceding dataset has some numerical features and some categorical features. Here, 53,940 is the exact number of samples that we have in this dataset. Now, for encoding the information in these categorical features, we use the one-hot encoding technique to transform these categorical features into dummy features. The reason behind this is because `scikit-learn` only works with numbers.

The following screenshot shows the lines of code used for the transformation of the categorical features to numbers:

```
In [4]:  print(diamonds['cut'].unique())
         print(diamonds['color'].unique())
         print(diamonds['clarity'].unique())

         ['Ideal' 'Premium' 'Good' 'Very Good' 'Fair']
         ['E' 'I' 'J' 'H' 'F' 'G' 'D']
         ['SI2' 'SI1' 'VS1' 'VS2' 'VVS2' 'VVS1' 'I1' 'IF']

In [5]:  diamonds = pd.concat([diamonds, pd.get_dummies(diamonds['cut'], prefix='cut', drop_first=True)],axis=1)
         diamonds = pd.concat([diamonds, pd.get_dummies(diamonds['color'], prefix='color', drop_first=True)],axis=1)
         diamonds = pd.concat([diamonds, pd.get_dummies(diamonds['clarity'], prefix='clarity', drop_first=True)],axis=1)
         diamonds.drop(['cut','color','clarity'], axis=1, inplace=True)
```

Here, we can see how we can do this with the `get_dummies` function from `pandas`. The final dataset looks similar to the one in the following screenshot:

```
In [6]:  diamonds.head()
Out[6]:
```

	carat	depth	table	price	x	y	z	cut_Good	cut_Ideal	cut_Premium	...	color_H
0	0.23	61.5	55.0	326	3.95	3.98	2.43	0	1	0	...	0
1	0.21	59.8	61.0	326	3.89	3.84	2.31	0	0	1	...	0
2	0.23	56.9	65.0	327	4.05	4.07	2.31	1	0	0	...	0
3	0.29	62.4	58.0	334	4.20	4.23	2.63	0	0	1	...	0
4	0.31	63.3	58.0	335	4.34	4.35	2.75	1	0	0	...	0

5 rows × 24 columns

Here, for each of the categories in the categorical variable, we have dummy features. The value here is `1` when the category is present and `0` when the category is not present in the particular diamond.

Now, for rescaling the data, we will use the `RobustScaler` method to transform all the features to a similar scale.

The following screenshot shows the lines of code used for importing the `train_test_split` function and the `RobustScaler` method:

```
In [7]:  from sklearn.model_selection import train_test_split
         from sklearn.metrics import mean_squared_error
         from sklearn.preprocessing import RobustScaler

In [8]:  target_name = 'price'
         robust_scaler = RobustScaler()
         X = diamonds.drop('price', axis=1)
         feature_names = X.columns
         X = robust_scaler.fit_transform(X)
         y = diamonds[target_name]
         X_train, X_test, y_train, y_test = train_test_split(X, y, test_size=0.2, random_state=55)
```

Here, we extract the features in the `X` matrix, mention the target, and then use the `train_test_split` function from `scikit-learn` to partition the data into two sets.

Training different regression models

The following screenshot shows the dataframe that we will use to record the metrics and the performance metrics that we will use for these models. Since this is a regression task, we will use the mean squared error. Here, in the columns, we have the four models that we will use. We will be using the KNN, Bagging, RandomForest, and Boosting variables:

```
In [9]:  models = pd.DataFrame(index=['train_mse', 'test_mse'],
                           columns=['KNN', 'Bagging', 'RandomForest', 'Boosting'])
```

KNN model

The **K-Nearest Neighbours** (**KNN**) model is not an ensemble learning model, but it performs the best among the simple models:

```
In [10]:  # 1. Import the estimator object (model)
          from sklearn.neighbors import KNeighborsRegressor
          # 2. Create an instance of the estimator
          knn = KNeighborsRegressor(n_neighbors=20, weights='distance', metric='euclidean', n_jobs=-1)
          # 3. Use the trainning data to train the estimator
          knn.fit(X_train, y_train)
          # 4. Evaluate the model
          models.loc['train_mse','KNN'] = mean_squared_error(y_pred=knn.predict(X_train),
                                                   y_true=y_train)

          models.loc['test_mse','KNN'] = mean_squared_error(y_pred=knn.predict(X_test),
                                                   y_true=y_test)
```

In the preceding model, we can see the process used while making a KNN. We will use 20 neighbors. We are using the euclidean metric to measure the distances between the points, and then we will train the model. Here, the performance metric is saved since the value is just 1, which is the mean squared error.

Bagging model

Bagging is an ensemble learning model. Any estimator can be used with the bagging method. So, let's take a case where we use KNN, as shown in the following screenshot:

```
In [11]:  # 1. Import the estimator object (model)
          from sklearn.ensemble import BaggingRegressor
          # 2. Create an instance of the estimator
          knn_for_bagging = KNeighborsRegressor(n_neighbors=20, weights='distance', metric='euclidean')

          bagging = BaggingRegressor(base_estimator=knn_for_bagging, n_estimators=15, max_features=0.75,
                                     random_state=55, n_jobs=-1)
          # 3. Use the trainning data to train the estimator
          bagging.fit(X_train, y_train)
          # 4. Evaluate the model
          models.loc['train_mse','Bagging'] = mean_squared_error(y_pred=bagging.predict(X_train),
                                                                 y_true=y_train)

          models.loc['test_mse','Bagging'] = mean_squared_error(y_pred=bagging.predict(X_test),
                                                                y_true=y_test)
```

Using the `n_estimators` parameter, we can produce an ensemble of 15 individual estimators. As a result, this will produce 15 bootstrap samples of the training dataset, and then, in each of these samples, it will fit one of these KNN regressors with 20 neighbors. In the end, we will get the individual predictions by using the bagging method. The method that this algorithm uses for giving individual predictions is a majority vote.

Random forests model

Random forests is another ensemble learning model. Here, we get all the ensemble learning objects from the `ensemble` submodule in `scikit-learn`. For example, here, we use the `RandomForestRegressor` method. The following screenshot, shows the algorithm used for this model:

```
In [12]:  # 1. Import the estimator object (model)
          from sklearn.ensemble import RandomForestRegressor
          # 2. Create an instance of the estimator
          RF = RandomForestRegressor(n_estimators=50, max_depth=16, random_state=55, n_jobs=-1)
          # 3. Use the trainning data to train the estimator
          RF.fit(X_train, y_train)
          # 4. Evaluate the model
          models.loc['train_mse','RandomForest'] = mean_squared_error(y_pred=RF.predict(X_train),
                                                       y_true=y_train)

          models.loc['test_mse','RandomForest'] = mean_squared_error(y_pred=RF.predict(X_test),
                                                      y_true=y_test)
```

So, in a case where we produce a forest of 50 individual predictors, this algorithm will produce 50 individual trees. Each tree will have `max_depth` of `16`, which will then produce the individual predictions again by majority vote.

Boosting model

Boosting is also an ensemble learning model. Here, we are using the `AdaBoostRegressor` model, and we will again produce `50` estimators. The following screenshot shows the algorithm used for this model:

```
In [13]:  # 1. Import the estimator object (model)
          from sklearn.ensemble import AdaBoostRegressor
          # 2. Create an instance of the estimator
          boosting = AdaBoostRegressor(n_estimators=50, learning_rate=0.05, random_state=55)
          # 3. Use the trainning data to train the estimator
          boosting.fit(X_train, y_train)
          # 4. Evaluate the model
          models.loc['train_mse','Boosting'] = mean_squared_error(y_pred=boosting.predict(X_train),
                                                   y_true=y_train)

          models.loc['test_mse','Boosting'] = mean_squared_error(y_pred=boosting.predict(X_test),
                                                  y_true=y_test)
```

The following screenshot shows the `train_mse` and `test_mse` results that we get after training all these models:

```
In [14]:  models

Out[14]:
                          KNN    Bagging    RandomForest    Boosting

           train_mse    78.503    112862          142186    1.82036e+06

            test_mse    744451    688060          376764    1.81305e+06
```

The following screenshot shows the algorithm and gives the comparison of all of these models on the basis of the values of the test mean squared error. The result is shown with the help of a horizontal bar graph:

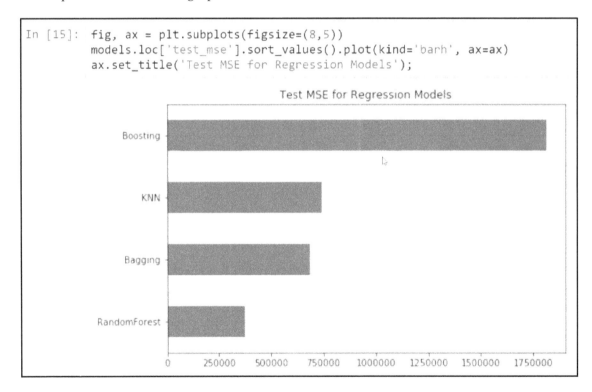

```
In [15]:  fig, ax = plt.subplots(figsize=(8,5))
          models.loc['test_mse'].sort_values().plot(kind='barh', ax=ax)
          ax.set_title('Test MSE for Regression Models');
```

Now, when we compare the result of all of these models, we can see that the random forest model is the most successful. The bagging and KNN models come second and third, respectively. This is why we use the KNN model with the bagging model.

The following screenshot shows the algorithm used to produce a graphical representation between the predicted prices and the observed prices while testing the dataset, and also shows the performance of the random forest model:

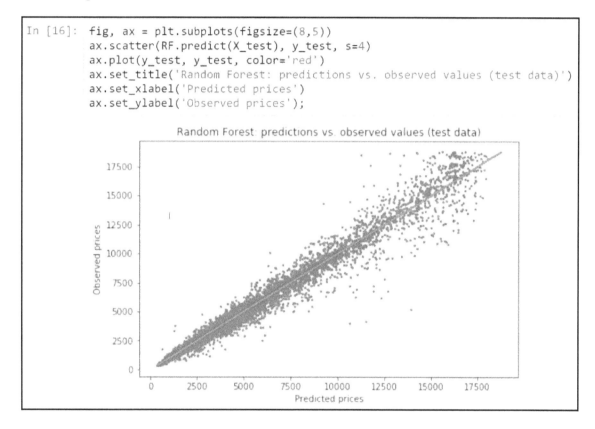

On using this model again with a `predict` API or with a `predict` method, we can get individual predictions.

For example, let's predict the values for the first ten predictions that we get from the testing dataset. The following algorithm shows the prediction that is made by this random forest model, which in turns shows us the real price and the predicted price of the diamonds that we have from the testing dataset:

```
In [18]:  n_pred=10
          ind_pred = RF.predict(X_test[:n_pred,])
          print('Real price, Predicted price:')
          for i, pred in enumerate(ind_pred):
              print(round(y_test.values[i]), round(pred), sep=', ')

          Real price, Predicted price:
          1882, 1784.0
          9586, 9592.0
          5058, 4907.0
          2780, 2666.0
          2811, 2612.0
          644, 660.0
          1378, 1420.0
          552, 572.0
          7823, 7817.0
          12800, 13046.0
```

From this screenshot, we can see that the values for `Real price` and `Predicted price` are very close, both for the expensive and inexpensive diamonds.

Using ensemble methods for classification

We are now familiar with the basic concept of ensemble learning and ensemble methods. Now, we will actually put these methods into use in building models using various machine learning algorithms and compare the results generated by them. To actually test all of these methods, we will need a sample dataset in order to implement these methods on the given dataset and see how this helps us with the performance of our models.

Predicting a credit card dataset

Let's take an example of a credit card dataset. This dataset comes from a financial institution in Taiwan and can be found here: `https://www.kaggle.com/uciml/default-of-credit-card-clients-dataset`. Take a look at the following screenshot, which shows you the dataset's information and its features:

Data Set Information:

This research aimed at the case of customers default payments in Taiwan

Features description:

- LIMIT_BAL: Amount of the given credit (NT dollar): it includes both the individual consumer credit and his/her family (supplementary) credit.
- SEX: Gender (1 = male; 2 = female).
- EDUCATION: Education (1 = graduate school; 2 = university; 3 = high school; 4 = others).
- MARRIAGE: Marital status (1 = married; 2 = single; 3 = others).
- AGE: Age (year).
- PAY_0 - PAY_6: History of past payment. We tracked the past monthly payment records (from April to September, 2005) as follows: 0 = the repayment status in September, 2005; 1 = the repayment status in August, 2005; . . .; 6 = the repayment status in April, 2005. The measurement scale for the repayment status is: -1 = pay duly; 1 = payment delay for one month; 2 = payment delay for two months; . . .; 8 = payment delay for eight months; 9 = payment delay for nine months and above.
- BILL_AMT1-BILL_AMT6: Amount of bill statement (NT dollar). X12 = amount of bill statement in September, 2005; X13 = amount of bill statement in August, 2005; . . .; X17 = amount of bill statement in April, 2005.
- PAY_AMT1-PAY_AMT6: Amount of previous payment (NT dollar).
- default payment next month: **positive class: default | negative class: pay**

Here, we have the following detailed information about each customer:

- It contains the limit balance, that is, the credit limit provided to the customer that is using the credit card
- Then, we have a few features regarding personal information about each customer, such as gender, education, marital status, and age
- We also have a history of past payments
- We also have the bill statement's amount
- We have the history of the bill's amount and previous payment amounts from the previous month up to six months prior, which was done by the customer

With this information, we are going to predict next month's payment status of the customer. We will first do a little transformation on these features to make them easier to interpret.

In this case, the positive class will be the default, so the number 1 represents the customers that fall under the default status category and the number 0 represents the customers who have paid their credit card dues.

Now, before we start, we need to import the required libraries by running a few commands, as shown in the following code snippet:

```
import numpy as np
import matplotlib.pyplot as plt
import pandas as pd
%matplotlib inline
```

The following screenshot shows the line of code that was used to prepare the credit card dataset:

Data Preparation

```
In [2]:  default = pd.read_csv('../data/credit_card_default.csv', index_col="ID")
         default.rename(columns=lambda x: x.lower(), inplace=True)
         default.rename(columns={'pay_0':'pay_1','default payment next month':'default'}, inplace=True)
         # Base values: female, other_education, not_married
         default['grad_school'] = (default['education'] == 1).astype('int')
         default['university'] = (default['education'] == 2).astype('int')
         default['high_school'] = (default['education'] == 3).astype('int')
         default['male'] = (default['sex']==1).astype('int')
         default['married'] = (default['marriage'] == 1).astype('int')

         default.drop(['sex','marriage', 'education'], axis=1, inplace=True)

         # For pay_i features: if >0 then it means the customer was delayed i months ago
         pay_features = ['pay_' + str(i) for i in range(1,7)]
         for p in pay_features:
             default[p] = (default[p] > 0).astype(int)
```

Let's produce the dummy feature for education in grad _school, university, and high_school. Instead of using the word sex, use the male dummy feature, and instead of using marriage, let's use the married feature. This feature is given value of 1 when the person is married, and 0 otherwise. For the pay_1 feature, we will do a little simplification process. If we see a positive number here, it means that the customer was late in his/her payments for i months. This means that this customer with an ID of 1 delayed the payment for the first two months. We can see that, 3 months ago, he/she was not delayed on his/her payments. This is what the dataset looks like:

```
In [3]:  default.head()
Out[3]:
```

ID	limit_bal	age	pay_1	pay_2	pay_3	pay_4	pay_5	pay_6	bill_amt1	bill_amt2	...	pay_amt3	pay_amt4	pay_amt5
1	20000	24	1	1	0	0	0	0	3913	3102	...	0	0	0
2	120000	26	0	1	0	0	0	1	2682	1725	...	1000	1000	0
3	90000	34	0	0	0	0	0	0	29239	14027	...	1000	1000	1000
4	50000	37	0	0	0	0	0	0	46990	48233	...	1200	1100	1069
5	50000	57	0	0	0	0	0	0	8617	5670	...	10000	9000	689

5 rows × 26 columns

Before fitting our models, the last thing we will do is rescale all the features because, as we can see here, we have features that are in very different scales. For example, limit_bal is in a very different scale than age.

This is why we will be using the RobustScaler method from scikit-learn—to try and transform all the features to a similar scale:

Building models using all features

```
In [4]: from sklearn.model_selection import train_test_split
        from sklearn.metrics import accuracy_score, precision_score, recall_score, confusion_matrix, precision_
        from sklearn.preprocessing import RobustScaler

In [5]: target_name = 'default'
        X = default.drop('default', axis=1)
        feature_names = X.columns
        robust_scaler = RobustScaler()
        X = robust_scaler.fit_transform(X)
        y = default[target_name]
        X_train, X_test, y_train, y_test = train_test_split(X, y, test_size=0.15, random_state=55, stratify=y)
```

As we can see in the preceding screenshot in the last line of code, we are partitioning our dataset into a training set and a testing set and below that, the CMatrix function is used to print the confusion matrix for each model. This function is explained in the following code snippet:

```
def CMatrix(CM, labels=['pay', 'default']):
    df = pd.DataFrame(data=CM, index=labels, columns=labels)
    df.index.name='TRUE'
    df.columns.name='PREDICTION'
    df.loc['Total'] = df.sum()
    df['Total'] = df.sum(axis=1)
    return df
```

Training different regression models

The following screenshot shows a dataframe where we are going to save performance. We are going to run four models, namely logistic regression, bagging, random forest, and boosting:

We are going to use the following evaluation metrics in this case:

- `accuracy`: This metric measures how often the model predicts defaulters and non-defaulters correctly
- `precision`: This metric will be when the model predicts the default and how often the model is correct
- `recall`: This metric will be the proportion of actual defaulters that the model will correctly predict

The most important of these is the `recall` metric. The reason behind this is that we want to maximize the proportion of actual defaulters that the model identifies, and so the model with the best recall is selected.

Logistic regression model

As in `scikit-learn`, we just import the object and then instantiate the estimator, and then pass training set X and training set Y to the `fit()` method. First, we will predict the test dataset and then produce the accuracy, precision, and recall scores. The following screenshot shows the code and the confusion matrix as the output:

```
In [8]:   # 1. Import the estimator object (model)
          from sklearn.linear_model import LogisticRegression

          # 2. Create an instance of the estimator
          logistic_regression = LogisticRegression(random_state=55)

          # 3. Use the trainning data to train the estimator
          logistic_regression.fit(X_train, y_train)

          # 4. Evaluate the model
          y_pred_test = logistic_regression.predict(X_test)
          metrics.loc['accuracy','LogisticReg'] = accuracy_score(y_pred=y_pred_test, y_true=y_test)
          metrics.loc['precision','LogisticReg'] = precision_score(y_pred=y_pred_test, y_true=y_test)
          metrics.loc['recall','LogisticReg'] = recall_score(y_pred=y_pred_test, y_true=y_test)
          #Confusion matrix
          CM = confusion_matrix(y_pred=y_pred_test, y_true=y_test)
          CMatrix(CM)
```

Out[8]:

PREDICTION	pay	default	Total
TRUE			
pay	3315	190	3505
default	684	311	995
Total	3999	501	4500

Later, we will save these into our `pandas` dataframe that we just created.

Bagging model

Training the bagging model using methods from the ensemble learning techniques involves importing the bagging classifier with the logistic regression methods. For this, we will fit 10 of these logistic regression models and then we will combine the 10 individual predictions into a single prediction using bagging. After that, we will save this into our metrics dataframe.

The following screenshot shows the code and the confusion matrix as the output:

```
In [9]:  # 1. Import the estimator object (model)
         from sklearn.ensemble import BaggingClassifier

         # 2. Create an instance of the estimator
         log_reg_for_bagging = LogisticRegression()
         bagging = BaggingClassifier(base_estimator=log_reg_for_bagging, n_estimators=10,
                                     random_state=55, n_jobs=-1)

         # 3. Use the trainning data to train the estimator
         bagging.fit(X_train, y_train)

         # 4. Evaluate the model
         y_pred_test = bagging.predict(X_test)
         metrics.loc['accuracy','Bagging'] = accuracy_score(y_pred=y_pred_test, y_true=y_test)
         metrics.loc['precision','Bagging'] = precision_score(y_pred=y_pred_test, y_true=y_test)
         metrics.loc['recall','Bagging'] = recall_score(y_pred=y_pred_test, y_true=y_test)
         #Confusion matrix
         CM = confusion_matrix(y_pred=y_pred_test, y_true=y_test)
         CMatrix(CM)
```

```
Out[9]:
```

PREDICTION	pay	default	Total
TRUE			
pay	3312	193	3505
default	683	312	995
Total	3995	505	4500

Random forest model

To perform classification with the random forest model, we have to import the `RandomForestClassifier` method. For example, let's take 35 individual trees with a `max_depth` of 20 for each tree. The `max_features` parameter tells `scikit-learn` that, when deciding upon the best split among possible features, we should use the square root of the total number of features that we have. These are all hyperparameters that we can tune.

The following screenshot shows the code and the confusion matrix as the output:

```
In [10]:  # 1. Import the estimator object (model)
          from sklearn.ensemble import RandomForestClassifier

          # 2. Create an instance of the estimator
          RF = RandomForestClassifier(n_estimators=35, max_depth=20, random_state=55, max_features='sqrt',
                                      n_jobs=-1)

          # 3. Use the trainning data to train the estimator
          RF.fit(X_train, y_train)

          # 4. Evaluate the model
          y_pred_test = RF.predict(X_test)
          metrics.loc['accuracy','RandomForest'] = accuracy_score(y_pred=y_pred_test, y_true=y_test)
          metrics.loc['precision','RandomForest'] = precision_score(y_pred=y_pred_test, y_true=y_test)
          metrics.loc['recall','RandomForest'] = recall_score(y_pred=y_pred_test, y_true=y_test)
          #Confusion matrix
          CM = confusion_matrix(y_pred=y_pred_test, y_true=y_test)
          CMatrix(CM)
Out[10]:
```

PREDICTION	pay	default	Total
TRUE			
pay	3276	229	3505
default	625	370	995
Total	3901	599	4500

Boosting model

In classification with the boosting model, we'll use the AdaBoostClassifier object. Here, we'll also use 50 estimators to combine the individual predictions. The learning rate that we will use here is 0.1, which is another hyperparameter for this model.

The following screenshot shows the code and the confusion matrix:

```
In [11]:  # 1. Import the estimator object (model)
          from sklearn.ensemble import AdaBoostClassifier

          # 2. Create an instance of the estimator
          boosting = AdaBoostClassifier(n_estimators=50, learning_rate=0.1, random_state=55)

          # 3. Use the trainning data to train the estimator
          boosting.fit(X_train, y_train)

          # 4. Evaluate the model
          y_pred_test = boosting.predict(X_test)
          metrics.loc['accuracy','Boosting'] = accuracy_score(y_pred=y_pred_test, y_true=y_test)
          metrics.loc['precision','Boosting'] = precision_score(y_pred=y_pred_test, y_true=y_test)
          metrics.loc['recall','Boosting'] = recall_score(y_pred=y_pred_test, y_true=y_test)
          #Confusion matrix
          CM = confusion_matrix(y_pred=y_pred_test, y_true=y_test)
          CMatrix(CM)
```

Out[11]:

PREDICTION	pay	default	Total
TRUE			
pay	3347	158	3505
default	724	271	995
Total	4071	429	4500

Now, we will compare the four models as shown in the following screenshot:

```
In [12]:  100*metrics
```

Out[12]:

	LogisticReg	Bagging	RandomForest	Boosting
accuracy	80.5778	80.5333	81.0222	80.4
precision	62.0758	61.7822	61.7696	63.1702
recall	31.2563	31.3568	37.1859	27.2362

The preceding screenshot shows the similar accuracies for the four models, but the most important metric for this particular application is the `recall` metric.

The following screenshot shows that the model with the best recall and accuracy is the random forest model:

```
In [13]:  fig, ax = plt.subplots(figsize=(8,5))
          metrics.plot(kind='barh', ax=ax)
          ax.grid();
```

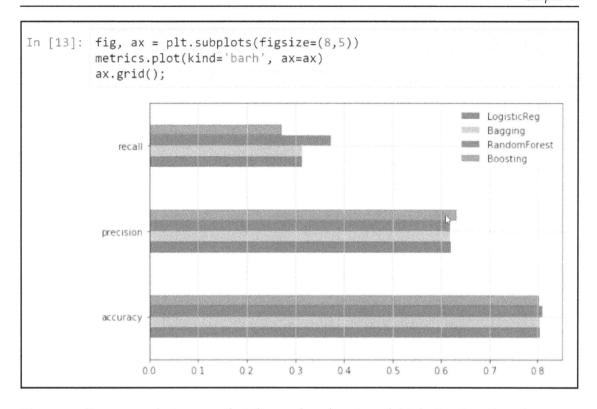

The preceding screenshot proves that the random forest model is better than the other models overall.

To see the relationship between precision, recall, and threshold, we can use the precision_recall_curve function from scikit-learn. Here, pass the predictions and the real observed values, and the result we get consists of the objects that will allow us to produce the code for the precision_recall_curve function.

The following screenshot shows the code for the precision_recall_curve function from scikit-learn:

```
In [14]:  precision_rf, recall_rf, thresholds_rf = precision_recall_curve(y_true=y_test,
                                                      probas_pred=RF.predict_proba(X_test)[:,
          precision_lr, recall_lr, thresholds_lr = precision_recall_curve(y_true=y_test,
                                                      probas_pred=logistic_regression.predict
```

The following screenshot will now visualize the relationship between precision and recall when using the random forest model and the logistic regression model:

```
In [15]: fig, ax = plt.subplots(figsize=(8,5))
         ax.plot(precision_rf, recall_rf, label='Random Forest')
         ax.plot(precision_lr,recall_lr , label='Logistic Regression')
         ax.set_ylim(0.5,1)
         ax.set_xlim(0.2,0.6)
         ax.set_xlabel('Precision')
         ax.set_ylabel('Recall')
         ax.set_title('Random Forest vs. Logistic Regression')
         ax.legend()
         ax.grid();
```

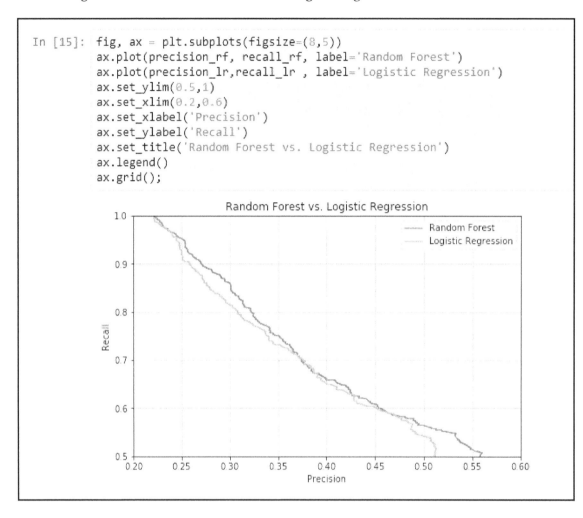

The preceding screenshot shows that the random forest model is better because it is above the logistic regression curve. So, for a precision of `0.30`, we get more recall with the random forest model than the logistic regression model.

To see the performance of the `RandomForestClassifier` method, we change the classification threshold. For example, we set a classification threshold of `0.12`, so we will get a precision of `30` and a recall of `84`. This model will correctly predict **84%** of the possible defaulters, which will be very useful for a financial institution. This shows that the boosting model is better than the logistic regression model for this.

The following screenshot shows the code and the confusion matrix:

```
In [28]:  y_pred_proba = RF.predict_proba(X_test)[:,1]
          y_pred_test = (y_pred_proba >= 0.12).astype('int')
          #Confusion matrix
          CM = confusion_matrix(y_pred=y_pred_test, y_true=y_test)
          print("Recall: ", 100*round(recall_score(y_pred=y_pred_test, y_true=y_test),2))
          print("Precision: ", 100*round(precision_score(y_pred=y_pred_test, y_true=y_test),2))
          CMatrix(CM)

          Recall:  84.0
          Precision:  30.0

Out[28]:
```

PREDICTION	pay	default	Total
TRUE			
pay	1601	1904	3505
default	160	835	995
Total	1761	2739	4500

Feature importance is something very important that we get while using a random forest model. The `scikit-learn` library calculates this metric of feature importance for each of the features that we use in our model. The internal calculation allows us to get a metric for the importance of each feature in the predictions.

The following screenshot shows the visualization of these features, hence highlighting the importance of using a `RandomForestClassifier` method:

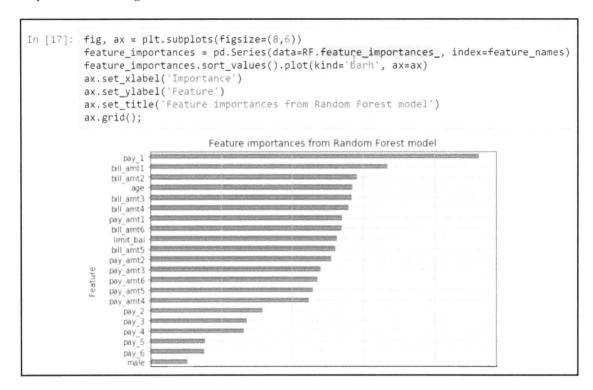

```
In [17]:  fig, ax = plt.subplots(figsize=(8,6))
          feature_importances = pd.Series(data=RF.feature_importances_, index=feature_names)
          feature_importances.sort_values().plot(kind='barh', ax=ax)
          ax.set_xlabel('Importance')
          ax.set_ylabel('Feature')
          ax.set_title('Feature importances from Random Forest model')
          ax.grid();
```

The most important feature for predicting whether the customer will default next month or whether the customer defaulted the month before is `pay_1`. Here, we just have to verify whether the customer paid last month or not. The other important features of this model are the bill amounts of two months, while the other feature in terms of importance is age.

The features that are not important for predicting the target are gender, marital status, and the education level of the customer.

Overall, the random forest model has proved to be better than the logistic regression model.

According to the no free lunch theorem, there is no single model that works best for every problem in every dataset. This means that ensemble learning cannot always outperform simpler methods because sometimes simpler methods perform better than complex methods. So, for every machine learning problem, we must use simple methods over complex methods and then evaluate the performance of both approaches to get the best results.

Summary

In this chapter, we introduced different ensemble methods such as bootstrap sampling, bagging, random forest, and boosting, and their working was explained with the help of some examples. We then used them for regression and classification. For regression, we took the example of a diamond dataset, and we also trained some KNN and other regression models. Later, their performance was compared. For classification, we took the example of a credit card dataset. Again, we trained all of the regression models. We compared their performance, and we found that the random forest model was the best performer.

In the next chapter, we will study k-fold cross-validation and parameter tuning. We will compare different ensemble learning models with k-fold cross-validation and later, we'll use k-fold cross-validation for hyperparameter tuning.

2
Cross-validation and Parameter Tuning

Predictive analytics is about making predictions for unknown events. We use it to produce models that generalize data. For this, we use a technique called cross-validation.

Cross-validation is a validation technique for assessing the result of a statistical analysis that generalizes to an independent dataset that gives a measure of out-of-sample accuracy. It achieves the task by averaging over several random partitions of the data into training and test samples. It is often used for hyperparameter tuning by doing cross-validation for several possible values of a parameter and choosing the parameter value that gives the lowest cross-validation average error.

There are two kinds of cross-validation: exhaustive and non-exhaustive. K-fold is an example of non-exhaustive cross-validation. It is a technique for getting a more accurate assessment of the model's performance. Using k-fold cross-validation, we can do hyperparameter tuning. This is about choosing the best hyperparameters for our models. Techniques such as k-fold cross-validation and hyperparameter tuning are crucial for building great predictive analytics models. There are many flavors or methods of cross-validation, such as holdout cross-validation and k-fold cross-validation.

In this chapter, we are going to cover the following topics:

- Holdout cross-validation
- K-fold cross-validation
- Comparing models with k-fold cross-validation
- Introduction to hyperparameter tuning

Holdout cross-validation

In holdout cross-validation, we hold out a percentage of observations and so we get two datasets. One is called the training dataset and the other is called the testing dataset. Here, we use the testing dataset to calculate our evaluation metrics, and the rest of the data is used to train the model. This is the process of holdout cross-validation.

The main advantage of holdout cross-validation is that it is very easy to implement and it is a very intuitive method of cross-validation.

The problem with this kind of cross-validation is that it provides a single estimate for the evaluation metric of the model. This is problematic because some models rely on randomness. So in principle, it is possible that the evaluation metrics calculated on the test sometimes they will vary a lot because of random chance. So the main problem with holdout cross-validation is that we get only one estimation of our evaluation metric.

K-fold cross-validation

In k-fold cross-validation, we basically do holdout cross-validation many times. So in k-fold cross-validation, we partition the dataset into *k* equal-sized samples. Of these many *k* subsamples, a single subsample is retained as the validation data for testing the model, and the remaining *k−1* subsamples are used as training data. This cross-validation process is then repeated *k* times, with each of the *k* subsamples used exactly once as the validation data. The *k* results can then be averaged to produce a single estimation.

The following screenshot shows a visual example of 5-fold cross-validation (*k=5*) :

5-fold CV	DATASET				
Estimation 1	Test	Train	Train	Train	Train
Estimation 2	Train	Test	Train	Train	Train
Estimation 3	Train	Train	Test	Train	Train
Estimation 4	Train	Train	Train	Test	Train
Estimation 5	Train	Train	Train	Train	Test

Here, we see that our dataset gets divided into five parts. We use the first part for testing and the rest for training.

The following are the steps we follow in the 5-fold cross-validation method:

1. We get the first estimation of our evaluation metrics.
2. We use the second part for testing and the rest for training, and we use that to get a second estimation of our evaluation metrics.
3. We use the third part for testing and the rest for training, and so on. In this way, we get five estimations of the evaluation metrics.

In k-fold cross-validation, after the k estimations of the evaluation matrix have been observed, an average of them is taken. This will give us a better estimation of the performance of the model. So, instead of having just one estimation of this evaluation metric, we can get n number of estimations with k-fold cross-validation, and then we can take the average and get a better estimation for the performance of the model.

As seen here, the advantage of the k-fold cross-validation method is that it can be used not only for model evaluation but also for hyperparameter tuning.

In this validation method, the common values for k are 5 and 10.

The following are the variants of k-fold cross-validation:

- **Repeated cross-validation:** In repeated cross-validation, we perform k-fold cross-validation many times. So, if we want 30 estimations of our evaluation metrics, we can do 5-fold cross-validation six times. So then we will get 30 estimations of our evaluation metrics.

- **Leave-One-Out (LOO) cross-validation:** In this method, we take the whole dataset for training except for one point. We use that one point for evaluation and then we repeat this process for every data point in our dataset.

If we have millions of points, this validation method will be really expensive computationally. We use repeated k-fold cross-validation in such cases, because this validation method will give us comparatively good results.

Implementing k-fold cross-validation

Let's take examples of a `diamond` dataset to understand the implementation of k-fold cross-validation.

For performing k-fold cross-validation in `scikit-learn`, we first have to import the libraries that we will use. The following code snippet shows the code used for importing the libraries:

```
import numpy as np
import matplotlib.pyplot as plt
import pandas as pd
%matplotlib inline
```

The second step is to prepare the dataset for the `diamond` dataset that we will use in this example. The following shows the code used to prepare data for this dataset:

```
# importing data
data_path= '../data/diamonds.csv'
diamonds = pd.read_csv(data_path)
diamonds = pd.concat([diamonds, pd.get_dummies(diamonds['cut'],
prefix='cut', drop_first=True)],axis=1)
diamonds = pd.concat([diamonds, pd.get_dummies(diamonds['color'],
prefix='color', drop_first=True)],axis=1)
diamonds = pd.concat([diamonds, pd.get_dummies(diamonds['clarity'],
prefix='clarity', drop_first=True)],axis=1)
diamonds.drop(['cut','color','clarity'], axis=1, inplace=True)
```

After preparing the data, we will create the objects used for modeling. The following shows the code used to create the objects for modeling:

```
from sklearn.preprocessing import RobustScaler
target_name = 'price'
robust_scaler = RobustScaler()
X = diamonds.drop('price', axis=1)
X = robust_scaler.fit_transform(X)
y = diamonds[target_name]
# Notice that we are not doing train-test split
#X_train, X_test, y_train, y_test = train_test_split(X, y, test_size=0.2,
random_state=55)
```

This is the same cell that we used in `Chapter 1`, *Ensemble Methods for Regression and Classification*. The difference here is that we are not using the `train_test_split` function. Here, we are producing the `X` matrix, which contains all the features and also has our target feature. So we have our `X` matrix and our `y` vector.

For training the model, we will instantiate our `RandomForestRegressor` function, which we found was the best model in `Chapter 1`, *Ensemble Methods for Regression and Classification*, for this dataset. The following shows the code used to instantiate the `RandomForestRegressor` function:

```
from sklearn.ensemble import RandomForestRegressor
RF = RandomForestRegressor(n_estimators=50, max_depth=16, random_state=123,
n_jobs=-1)
```

To perform k-fold cross-validation, we import the `cross_validate` function from the `model_selection` module in `scikit-learn`. The following shows the code used to import the `cross_validate` function:

```
# this will work from sklearn version 0.19, if you get an error
# make sure you upgrade: $conda upgrade scikit-learn
from sklearn.model_selection import cross_validate
```

This `cross_validate` function works as follows:

- We provide the estimator, which will be the `RandomForestRegressor` function. The following shows the code used to apply the `RandomForestRegressor` function:

  ```
  scores = cross_validate(estimator=RF,X=X,y=y,
  scoring=['mean_squared_error','r2'],
  cv=10, n_jobs=-1)
  ```

  Here, we pass the `X` object and the `y` object.

- We provide a set of metrics that we want to evaluate for this model and for this dataset. In this case, evaluation is done using the `mean_squared_error` function and the `r2` metrics, as shown in the preceding code. Here, we pass the value of *k* in `cv`. So, in this case, we will do tenfold cross-validation.

The output that we get from this `cross_validate` function will be a dictionary with the corresponding matrix. For better understanding, the output is converted into a dataframe. The following screenshot shows the code use to visualize the scores in the dataframe and the dataframe output:

```
In [7]:  scores = pd.DataFrame(scores)
         scores['test_mean_squared_error'] = -1*scores['test_mean_squared_error']
         scores['train_mean_squared_error'] = -1*scores['train_mean_squared_error']
         scores

Out[7]:
```

	fit_time	score_time	test_mean_squared_error	test_r2	train_mean_squared_error	train_r2
0	2.704191	0.720918	3.755390e+05	0.538764	148065.528065	0.991526
1	3.141356	0.988628	4.506041e+05	0.672636	150123.441197	0.991437
2	3.756991	1.060821	1.429308e+06	0.386105	118993.885068	0.993105
3	3.542923	1.004674	2.386801e+06	0.569107	121708.194620	0.992298
4	3.403554	1.176127	6.002576e+06	0.653763	84805.134870	0.990100
5	3.737440	0.910923	1.376623e+06	0.958366	134400.626049	0.990314
6	3.839710	4.791745	2.447721e+04	-0.314355	149193.566169	0.990960
7	5.881141	0.306817	6.405753e+04	-0.214988	149713.173174	0.991024
8	5.870614	0.363968	1.156133e+05	0.304016	156899.220946	0.990759
9	6.064633	0.298291	1.976350e+05	0.396521	154009.670050	0.991083

Here, we apply `test_mean_squared_error` and `test_r2`, which were the two metrics that we wanted to evaluate. After evaluating, we get the `train_mean_squared_error` value and the `test_r2` set. So, we are interested in the testing metrics.

To get a better assessment of the performance of a model, we will take an average (mean) of all of the individual measurements.

The following shows the code for getting the `Mean test MSE` and `Mean test R-squared` values and output showing their values:

```
print("Mean test MSE:", round(scores['test_mean_squared_error'].mean()))
print("Mean test R-squared:", scores['test_r2'].mean())
```

So here, on averaging, we see that the mean of the test MSE is the value that we have here and an average of the other metric, which was the R-squared evaluation metrics.

Comparing models with k-fold cross-validation

As k-fold cross-validation method proved to be a better method, it is more suitable for comparing models. The reason behind this is that k-fold cross-validation gives much estimation of the evaluation metrics, and on averaging these estimations, we get a better assessment of model performance.

The following shows the code used to import libraries for comparing models:

```
import numpy as np
import matplotlib.pyplot as plt
import pandas as pd
%matplotlib inline
```

After importing libraries, we'll import the `diamond` dataset. The following shows the code used to prepare this `diamond` dataset:

```
# importing data
data_path= '../data/diamonds.csv'
diamonds = pd.read_csv(data_path)
diamonds = pd.concat([diamonds, pd.get_dummies(diamonds['cut'],
prefix='cut', drop_first=True)],axis=1)
diamonds = pd.concat([diamonds, pd.get_dummies(diamonds['color'],
prefix='color', drop_first=True)],axis=1)
diamonds = pd.concat([diamonds, pd.get_dummies(diamonds['clarity'],
prefix='clarity', drop_first=True)],axis=1)
diamonds.drop(['cut','color','clarity'], axis=1, inplace=True)
```

Now, we have to prepare objects for modeling after preparing the dataset for doing model comparison. The following shows the code used for preparing the objects for modeling. Here we have the X matrix, showing the features, and the y vector, which is the target for this dataset:

```
from sklearn.preprocessing import RobustScaler
target_name = 'price'
robust_scaler = RobustScaler()
X = diamonds.drop('price', axis=1)
X = robust_scaler.fit_transform(X)
y = diamonds[target_name]
```

Here, we will compare the KNN model, the random forest model, and the bagging model. In these models, using tenfold cross-validation, we will use the `KNNRegressor`, `RandomForestRegressor`, and `AdaBoostRegressor` functions.

Then we will import the `cross_validate` function. The following shows the code used to import the `cross_validate` function for these three models:

```
from sklearn.neighbors import KNeighborsRegressor
from sklearn.ensemble import RandomForestRegressor
from sklearn.ensemble import AdaBoostRegressor
from sklearn.model_selection import cross_validate
```

The next step is to compare the models using the `cross_validate` function. The following shows the code block used for comparing these three models:

```
## KNN
knn = KNeighborsRegressor(n_neighbors=20, weights='distance',
metric='euclidean', n_jobs=-1)
knn_test_mse = cross_validate(estimator=knn,X=X,y=y,
 scoring='mean_squared_error',
 cv=10, n_jobs=-1)['test_score']

## Random Forests
RF = RandomForestRegressor(n_estimators=50, max_depth=16, random_state=55,
n_jobs=-1)
RF_test_mse = cross_validate(estimator=RF,X=X,y=y,
 scoring='mean_squared_error',
 cv=10, n_jobs=-1)['test_score']

## Boosting
boosting = AdaBoostRegressor(n_estimators=50, learning_rate=0.05,
random_state=55)
boosting_test_mse = cross_validate(estimator=boosting,X=X,y=y,
 scoring='mean_squared_error',
 cv=10, n_jobs=-1)['test_score']
```

Here, we see the result of the testing evaluation metrics that we will use for every model. We use the `mean_squared_error` function. For every model, we use tenfold cross-validation and after getting the result, we get the `test_score` variable. This `test_score` variable is the mean-squared error in this case, and is shown in the following code:

```
mse_models = -1*pd.DataFrame({'KNN':knn_test_mse,
 'RandomForest': RF_test_mse,
 'Boosting':boosting_test_mse})
```

The following screenshot shows the code for the result that we got after running the tenfold cross-validation for every model and also, the table showing the 10 estimations of the evaluation metrics for the three models:

```
In [7]:  mse_models

Out[7]:
                  Boosting            KNN   RandomForest

        0   1.871637e+06   6.261917e+05    3.751482e+05

        1   3.796796e+06   5.654357e+05    4.506298e+05

        2   2.928736e+06   1.172655e+06    1.413179e+06

        3   7.420615e+06   2.856918e+06    2.360007e+06

        4   1.004345e+07   1.346273e+07    5.753556e+06

        5   3.616306e+06   3.056937e+06    1.351211e+06

        6   3.880890e+04   4.662510e+04    2.460778e+04

        7   5.167800e+05   1.218936e+05    6.391719e+04

        8   6.208819e+05   2.427801e+05    1.190176e+05

        9   6.810013e+05   4.797159e+05    1.917342e+05
```

This table shows a lot of variation in estimations of every model. To know the actual performance of any model, we take the average of the result. So, in the preceding figure, we take the mean of all the values and then plot it.

The following screenshot shows the code used to take the mean and the graph showing the mean MSE values for every model:

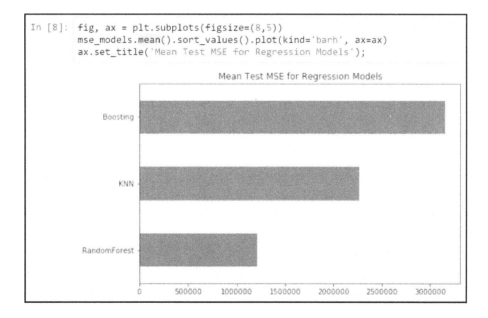

On averaging, the random forest model performs best out of the three models. So, after taking an average, the second place goes to the KNN model, and the boosting model takes last place.

The following figure shows the code used to get the box plot for these evaluation metrics and the box plot for the three models:

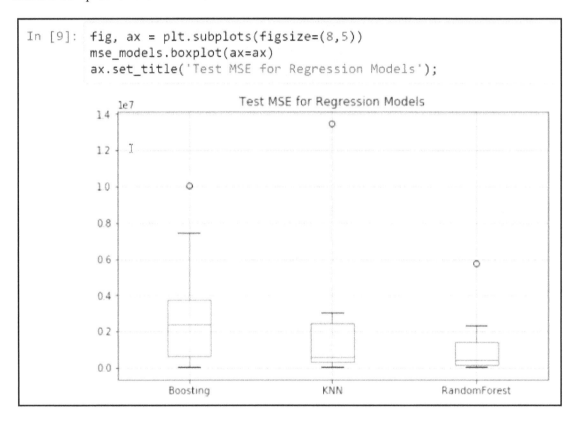

So, looking at the box plot for these evaluation metrics, we see that, the random forest performs the best.

To check the degree of variability of these models, we can analyze the standard deviation of the test MSE for regression models. The following screenshot shows the code used to check the degree of variability and the plot showing the standard deviation of these models:

```
In [10]:  fig, ax = plt.subplots(figsize=(8,5))
          mse_models.std().sort_values().plot(kind='barh', ax=ax)
          ax.set_title('Standard Deviation of Test MSE for Regression Models');
```

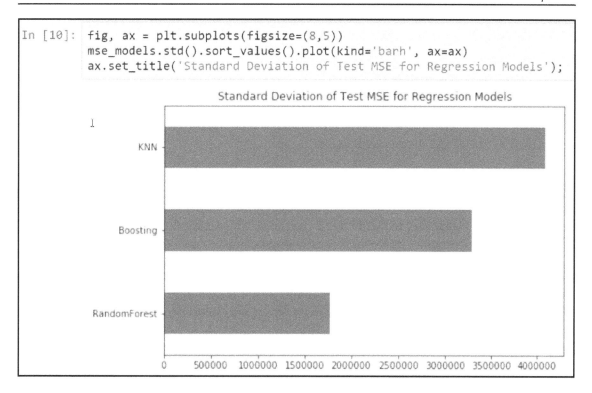

The preceding screenshot shows that the most variable model in this case was the KNN model, followed by the boosting model, and random forest model had the least variation. So, the random forest model is the best among these three models. Even for this dataset, the random forest model performs the best.

Introduction to hyperparameter tuning

The method used to choose the best estimators for a particular dataset or choosing the best values for all hyperparameters is called **hyperparameter tuning**. Hyperparameters are parameters that are not directly learned within estimators. Their value is decided by the modelers.

For example, in the `RandomForestClassifier` object, there are a lot of hyperparameters, such as `n_estimators`, `max_depth`, `max_features`, and `min_samples_split`. Modelers decide the values for these hyperparameters.

Exhaustive grid search

One of the most important and generally-used methods for performing hyperparameter tuning is called the **exhaustive grid search**. This is a brute-force approach because it tries all of the combinations of hyperparameters from a grid of parameter values. Then, for each combination of hyperparameters, the model is evaluated using k-fold cross-validation and any other specified metrics. So the combination that gives us the best metric is the one that is returned by the object that we will use in `scikit-learn`.

Let's take an example of a hyperparameter grid. Here, we try three different values, such as 10, 30, and 50, for the `n_estimators` hyperparameter. We will try two options, such as auto and square root, for `max_features`, and assign four values—5, 10, 20, and 30—for `max_depth`. So, in this case, we will have 24 hyperparameter combinations. These 24 will be evaluated. For every one of these 24 combinations, in this case, we use tenfold cross-validation and the computer will be training and evaluating 240 models. The biggest shortcoming that grid search faces is the curse of dimensionality which will be covered in the coming chapters. The curse of dimensionality essentially means that the number of times you will have to evaluate your model increases exponentially with the number of parameters.

If certain combinations of hyperparameters are not tested, then different grids can be passed to the `GridSearchCV` object. Here, different grids can be passed in the form of a list of dictionaries because every grid is a dictionary in `scikit-learn`.

 Don't ever use the entire dataset for tuning parameters, always perform train-test split when tuning parameters, otherwise the hyperparameters may be fit to that specific dataset and the model won't generalize well to new data.

So, we perform the train-test split and use one part of the dataset to learn the hyperparameters of our model; the part that we left for testing should be used for the final model evaluation, and later we use the whole dataset to fit the model.

Hyperparameter tuning in scikit-learn

Let's take an example of the `diamond` dataset to understand hyperparameter tuning in `scikit-learn`.

To perform hyperparameter tuning, we first have to import the libraries that we will use. To import the libraries, we will use the following code:

```
import numpy as np
import matplotlib.pyplot as plt
import pandas as pd
from sklearn.metrics import mean_squared_error
%matplotlib inline
```

Then, we perform the transformations to the `diamond` dataset that we will use in this example. The following shows the code used to prepare data for this dataset:

```
# importing data
data_path= '../data/diamonds.csv'
diamonds = pd.read_csv(data_path)
diamonds = pd.concat([diamonds, pd.get_dummies(diamonds['cut'],
prefix='cut', drop_first=True)],axis=1)
diamonds = pd.concat([diamonds, pd.get_dummies(diamonds['color'],
prefix='color', drop_first=True)],axis=1)
diamonds = pd.concat([diamonds, pd.get_dummies(diamonds['clarity'],
prefix='clarity', drop_first=True)],axis=1)
diamonds.drop(['cut','color','clarity'], axis=1, inplace=True)
```

After preparing the data, we will create the objects used for modeling. The following shows the code used to create the objects for modeling:

```
from sklearn.preprocessing import RobustScaler
from sklearn.model_selection import train_test_split
target_name = 'price'
robust_scaler = RobustScaler()
X = diamonds.drop('price', axis=1)
X = robust_scaler.fit_transform(X)
y = diamonds[target_name]
X_train, X_test, y_train, y_test = train_test_split(X, y, test_size=0.1,
random_state=123)
```

After performing and creating the objects used for modeling, we perform the `train_test_split` function. In the preceding codeblock, we will set 0.1(10%) of the data for testing, so this portion of the dataset will be used for model evaluation after tuning the hyperparameters.

We will tune the RandomForestRegressor model using the following parameters:

- n_estimators: This parameter represents the number of trees in the forest.
- max_features: This parameter represents the number of features to consider when looking for best split. The possible choices are n_features, which corresponds to the auto hyperparameter, or the square root of the log2 of the number of features.
- max_depth: This parameter represents the maximum depth of the tree.

Different values with a grid search will be used for these parameters. For n_estimators and max_depth, we will use four different values. For n_estimators, we will use [25,50,75,100] as values, and for max_depth, we will use [10,15,20,30] as values. For max_features, we will use the auto and square root.

Now we will instantiate the RandomForestRegressor model explicitly without any hyperparameters. The following shows the code used to instantiate it:

```
from sklearn.ensemble import RandomForestRegressor
RF = RandomForestRegressor(random_state=55, n_jobs=-1)
```

The parameter grid is basically a dictionary where we pass the name of the hyperparameter and the values that we want to try. The following code block shows the parameter grid with different parameters:

```
parameter_grid = {'n_estimators': [25,50,75,100],
'max_depth': [10,15,20,30],
'max_features': ['auto','sqrt']}
```

In total, we have four values for n_estimators, four values for max_depth, and two for max_features. So, on calculating, there are in total of 32 combinations of hyperparameters.

To perform hyperparameter tuning in scikit-learn, we will use the GridSearchCV object. The following shows the code used to import the object from scikit-learn:

```
from sklearn.model_selection import GridSearchCV
```

Here, we pass the estimator we want to tune, in this case, RandomForestRegressor. The following screenshot shows the code used and the output that we get:

```
In [7]:  RF_classifier = GridSearchCV(estimator=RF, param_grid=parameter_grid, refit=True,
                           scoring='mean_squared_error', cv=10, n_jobs=-1)

         RF_classifier.fit(X_train, y_train)                    ]

Out[7]:  GridSearchCV(cv=10, error_score='raise',
              estimator=RandomForestRegressor(bootstrap=True, criterion='mse', max_depth=None,
                  max_features='auto', max_leaf_nodes=None,
                  min_impurity_decrease=0.0, min_impurity_split=None,
                  min_samples_leaf=1, min_samples_split=2,
                  min_weight_fraction_leaf=0.0, n_estimators=10, n_jobs=-1,
                  oob_score=False, random_state=55, verbose=0, warm_start=False),
              fit_params=None, iid=True, n_jobs=-1,
              param_grid={'n_estimators': [25, 50, 75, 100], 'max_depth': [10, 15, 20, 30], 'max_features':
         ['auto', 'sqrt']},
              pre_dispatch='2*n_jobs', refit=True, return_train_score=True,
              scoring='mean_squared_error', verbose=0)
```

Then we pass the parameter grid that we want to try. Here, `refit` means that this estimator object will refit using the best parameters that it found using this process of grid-search and cross-validation. This is the evaluation metric that will be used by this object to evaluate all of the possible combinations of hyperparameters. In this case, we will use tenfold cross-validation. So after creating that, we can use the `fit` method and pass the training object. Since we are using tenfold cross-validation with 32 combinations, the model will evaluate 320 models.

We can get the results using the `cv _results_` attribute from the object that we created using the `GridSearchCV` method. The following screenshot shows the code used to get the result and output showing the result:

```
In [8]:  results - pd.DataFrame(RF_classifier.cv_results_)
         results.head[ ]

Out[8]:
```

	mean_fit_time	mean_score_time	mean_test_score	mean_train_score	param_max_depth	param_max_features	param_n_esti
0	1.513492	1.439769	-634506.134927	-528058.000445	10	auto	
1	7.872935	1.502697	-627471.180849	-522750.323802	10	auto	
2	10.642504	2.227475	-625250.042255	-520297.873599	10	auto	
3	13.102797	1.598602	-622589.325370	-517914.197711	10	auto	
4	2.363837	0.955541	-810008.883519	-695999.613338	10	sqrt	

Here, the most important thing is to get `best_params_`. So with `best_params_`, we can see the combination of parameters of all 32 combinations. The following screenshot shows the input used to get the parameters and the output showing combination of parameters that can give the best result:

```
In [10]:  RF_classifier.best_params_

Out[10]:  {'max_depth': 20, 'max_features': 'auto', 'n_estimators': 100}
```

Here, we can see that the combination that can give `best_params_` is `max_depth` with a value of 20, `max _features` with a value of auto, and `n_estimators` with a value of 100. So this is the best possible combination of parameters.

We can also get the `best_estimator_` object, and this is the complete list of hyperparameters. The following screenshot shows the code used to get `best_estimator_` and output showing the result:

```
In [12]:  RF_classifier.best_estimator_

Out[12]:  RandomForestRegressor(bootstrap=True, criterion='mse', max_depth=20,
                    max_features='auto', max_leaf_nodes=None,
                    min_impurity_decrease=0.0, min_impurity_split=None,
                    min_samples_leaf=1, min_samples_split=2,
                    min_weight_fraction_leaf=0.0, n_estimators=100, n_jobs=-1,
                    oob_score=False, random_state=55, verbose=0, warm_start=False)
```

So, as we tuned the hyperparameters of the random forest model, we got different values from the values that we got before; when we had values for `n_estimators` as 50, `max_depth` as 16, and `max_features` as auto, the parameters in that model were untuned.

Comparing tuned and untuned models

We can compare the best model that we got while tuning the parameters with the best model that we have been using without the help of tuning `n_estimators` with a value of 50, `max_depth` with a value of 16, and `max_features` as `auto`, and in both the cases it was random forest. The following code shows the values of the parameters of both the tuned and untuned models:

```
## Random Forests
RF_model1 = RandomForestRegressor(n_estimators=50, max_depth=16,
random_state=123, n_jobs=-1)
RF_model1.fit(X_train, y_train)
RF_model1_test_mse = mean_squared_error(y_pred=RF_model1.predict(X_test),
y_true=y_test)

## Random Forest with tunned parameters
RF_tunned_test_mse =
mean_squared_error(y_pred=RF_classifier.predict(X_test), y_true=y_test)
```

To actually see the comparison between the tuned and untuned models, we can see the value of the mean-square error. The following screenshot shows the code to get the `mean_squared_error` value for the two models, and the plot showing the comparison of the MSE value of the two models:

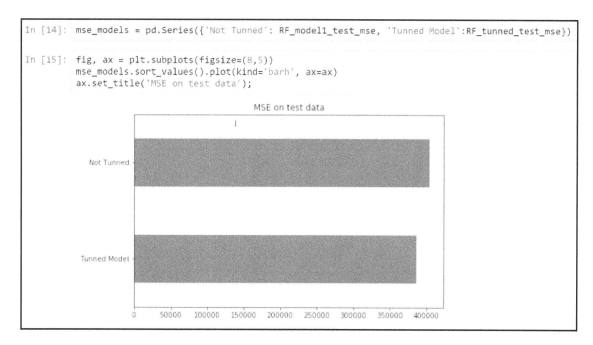

We can clearly observe here that, on comparison, these tuned parameters perform better than the untuned parameters in both of the random forest models.

To see the actual difference in values between the two models, we can do a little calculation. The following screenshot shows the calculation for getting the percentage of improvement and output showing the actual percentage value:

```
In [16]:  100*(RF_tunned_test_mse-RF_model1_test_mse)/RF_model1_test_mse

Out[16]:  -4.580267005058392
```

Here we got an improvement of 4.6% for the tuned model over the untuned one and this is actually very good. In these models, an improvement of 1%-3% percent can also have huge practical implications.

Summary

In this chapter, we learned about cross-validation, and different methods of cross-validation, including holdout cross-validation and k-fold cross-validation. We came to know that k-fold cross-validation is nothing but doing holdout cross-validation many times. We implemented k-fold cross-validation using the `diamond` dataset. We also compared different models using k-fold cross-validation and found the best-performing model, which was the random forest model.

Then, we discussed hyperparameter tuning. We came across the exhaustive grid-search method, which is used to perform hyperparameter tuning. We implemented hyperparameter tuning again using the `diamond` dataset. We also compared tuned and untuned models, and found that tuned parameters make the model perform better than untuned ones.

In the next chapter, we will study feature selection methods, dimensionality reduction and **principle component analysis** (**PCA**), and feature engineering. We will also learn about a method to improve the model with feature engineering.

3
Working with Features

In this chapter, we are going to take a close look at how features play an important role in the feature engineering technique. We'll learn some techniques that will allow us to improve our predictive analytics models in two ways: in terms of the performance metrics of our models and to understand the relationship between the features and the target variables that we are trying to predict.

In this chapter, we are going to cover the following topics:

- Feature selection methods
- Dimensionality reduction and PCA
- Creating new features
- Improving models with feature engineering

Feature selection methods

Feature selection methods are used for selecting features that are likely to help with predictions. The following are the three methods for feature selection:

- Removing dummy features with low variance
- Identifying important features statistically
- Recursive feature elimination

When building predictive analytics models, some features won't be related to the target and this will prove to be less helpful in prediction. Now, the problem is that including irrelevant features in the model can introduce noise and add bias to the model. So, feature selection techniques are a set of techniques used to select the most relevant and useful features that will help either with prediction or with understanding our model.

Removing dummy features with low variance

The first technique of feature selection that we will learn about is removing dummy features with low variance. The only transformation that we have been applying so far to our features is to transform the categorical features using the encoding technique. If we take one categorical feature and use this encoding technique, we get a set of dummy features, which are to be examined to see whether they have variability or not. So, features with a very low variance are likely to have little impact on prediction. Now, why is that? Imagine that you have a dataset where you have a gender feature and that 98% of the observations correspond to just the female gender. This feature won't have any impact on prediction because almost all of the cases are just of a single category, so there is not enough variability. These cases become candidates lined up for elimination and such features should be examined more carefully. Now, take a look at the following formula:

$$Var[X] = p(1 - p)$$

You can remove all dummy features that are either 0 or 1 in more than x% of the samples, or what you can do is to establish a minimum threshold for the variance of such features. Now, the variance of such features can be obtained with the preceding formula, where **p** is the number or the proportion of **1** in your dummy features. We will see how this works in a Jupyter Notebook.

Identifying important features statistically

This method will help you make use of some statistical tests for identifying and selecting relevant features. So, for example, for classification tasks we can use an ANOVA F-statistic to evaluate the relationship between numerical features and the target, which will be a categorical feature because this is an example of a classic task. Or, to evaluate the statistical relationship between a categorical feature and the target, we will use the chi-squared test to evaluate such a relationship. In `scikit-learn`, we can use the `SelectKBest` object and we will see how to use these objects in a Jupyter Notebook.

Recursive feature elimination

The process of identifying important features and removing the ones that we think are not important for our model is called **recursive feature elimination** (**RFE**). RFE can also be applied in `scikit-learn` and we can use this technique for calculating coefficients, such as linear, logistic regression, or with models to calculate something called **feature importance**. The random forests model provides us with those feature importance metrics. So, for models that don't calculate either coefficients or feature importance, these methods cannot be used; for example, for KNN models, you cannot apply the RFE technique because this begins by predefining the required features to use in your model. Using all features, this method fits the model and then, based on the coefficients or the feature importance, the least important features are eliminated. This procedure is recursively repeated on the selected set of features until the desired number of features to select is eventually reached.

There are the following few methods to select important features in your models:

- L1 feature
- Selection threshold methods
- Tree-based methods

Let's go to our Jupyter Notebook to see how we actually apply these methods in `scikit-learn`. The following screenshot depicts the necessary libraries and modules to import:

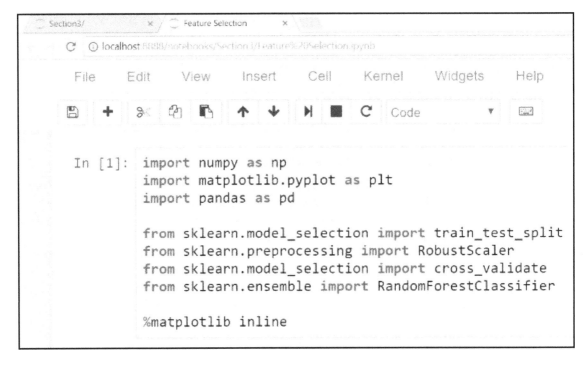

In the following screenshot, we have first used the credit card default dataset and we are applying the traditional transformations that we do to the raw data:

```
In [2]:  default = pd.read_csv('../data/credit_card_default.csv', index_col="ID")
         default.rename(columns=lambda x: x.lower(), inplace=True)
         default.rename(columns={'pay_0':'pay_1','default payment next month':'default'}, inplace=True)

         default['grad_school'] = (default['education'] == 1).astype(int)
         default['university'] = (default['education'] == 2).astype(int)
         default['high_school'] = (default['education'] == 3).astype(int)
         default.drop('education', axis=1, inplace=True)

         default['male'] = (default['sex']==1).astype(int)
         default['married'] = (default['marriage'] == 1).astype(int)
         default.drop(['sex','marriage'], axis=1, inplace=True)

         # For pay_n features if >0 then it means the customer was delayed on that month
         pay_features = ['pay_' + str(i) for i in range(1,7)]
         for p in pay_features:
             default[p] = (default[p] > 0).astype(int)
```

The following screenshot shows the dummy features that we have in our dataset and the
numerical features, depending on the type of feature:

```
In [3]:  dummy_features =['pay_'+str(i) for i in range(1,7)]
         dummy_features += ['male','married','grad_school','university','high_school']
         numerical_features = [x for x in default.columns if x not in dummy_features+['default']]
```

Here, we are applying the scaling operation for feature modeling:

```
In [4]:  target_name = 'default'
         X = default.drop('default', axis=1)
         feature_names = X.columns
         robust_scaler = RobustScaler()
         X = robust_scaler.fit_transform(X)
         y = default[target_name]
```

The first method that we talked about in the presentation was removing dummy features
with low variance to get the variances from our features using the var() method:

```
In [5]:  variances = pd.Series(default.var(axis=0))
```

Let's see the variances only for the dummy features; for example, a threshold for the variance will consider only the dummy features with a variance over 0.1. In that case, with such a threshold of 0.1, the two candidates for elimination, pay_5 and pay_6, would be the first few unnecessary dummy features with low variance that will be removed. Take a look at the following screenshot, which depicts the candidates for elimination:

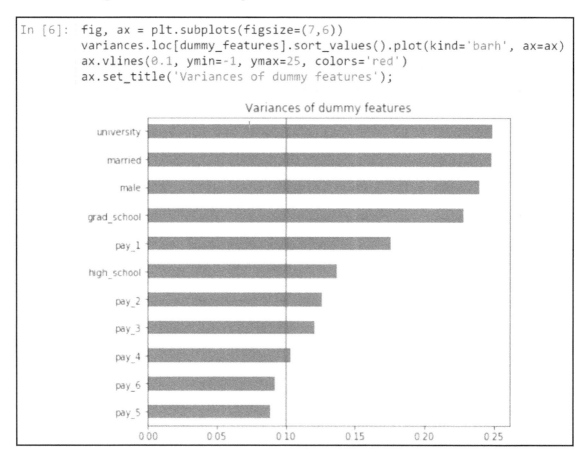

The second approach that we talked about is statistically selecting the features that are related to the target, and we have two cases, dummy features and numerical features.

Let's perform the statistical tests for the dummy features. We are going to import objects in the chi2 object from the feature_selection module in the scikit-learn library. We will also use the SelectKBest object to perform the statistical tests in all of the dummy features as shown in the following screenshot:

```
In [7]:  from sklearn.feature_selection import SelectKBest
         from sklearn.feature_selection import chi2
```

Here, we instantiate an object called dummy _selector and pass the required statistical test to apply to it. Here, we are passing the k ="all" argument because this statistical test is to be applied to all of the dummy features. After instantiating this object, the fit() method is called. Take a look at the following screenshot:

```
In [8]:  dummy_selector = SelectKBest(chi2, k="all")
         dummy_selector.fit(default[dummy_features], default[target_name])

Out[8]:  SelectKBest(k='all', score_func=<function chi2 at 0x00000214BF3E3EA0>)
```

In the following screenshot, we have the chi-squared scores. This isn't a statistical test and, the larger the number, the stronger the relationship between the feature and the target:

```
In [9]:  dummy_selector.scores_

Out[9]:  array([ 3141.39566361,  2920.6909149 ,  2222.60680108,  2010.51973814,
                 1926.49180212,  1630.3290955 ,    28.92210682,    14.48674466,
                   51.149551   ,    21.23797331,    26.33631512])
```

Now, if you remember your statistics class, this is a hypothesis testing setting. So, we can also calculate the p values and we can say that the features where pvalues_ is greater than 0.05 are not related to the target. Now, in this case, we get very small p values for all of the features, as shown in the following screenshot:

```
In [10]:  dummy_selector.pvalues_

Out[10]:  array([ 0.00000000e+00,  0.00000000e+00,  0.00000000e+00,
                  0.00000000e+00,  0.00000000e+00,  0.00000000e+00,
                  7.53480421e-08,  1.41149283e-04,  8.55902557e-13,
                  4.05647636e-06,  2.86844139e-07])
```

There is a relationship between the target and all of the dummy features, so under this methodology, we shouldn't eliminate any of these dummy features.

Now, we can use another statistical test called `f_ classif` to evaluate the relationship between numerical features and the target, as shown in the following screenshot:

```
In [11]:  # ANOVA F-value between label/feature for classification tasks.
          from sklearn.feature_selection import f_classif
```

Reusing this `f_classif` object, we will pass the required statistical tests and number of features. In this case, we want to apply the test to all numerical features and then use the `fit()` method again with the numerical features and the target:

```
In [12]:  num_selector = SelectKBest(f_classif, k="all")
          num_selector.fit(default[numerical_features], default[target_name])

Out[12]:  SelectKBest(k='all', score_func=<function f_classif at 0x00000214BF3E30D0>)
```

The p values that we receive from the application of this statistical test are shown in the following screenshot:

```
In [13]:  num_selector.pvalues_

Out[13]:  array([  1.30224395e-157,   1.61368459e-002,   6.67329549e-004,
                   1.39573624e-002,   1.47699827e-002,   7.85556416e-002,
                   2.41634443e-001,   3.52122521e-001,   1.14648761e-036,
                   3.16665676e-024,   1.84177029e-022,   6.83094160e-023,
                   1.24134477e-021,   3.03358907e-020])
```

We can pass the `f_classif` statistical test and then select the numerical features that have a p value greater than `0.05`, which is the usual threshold for statistical tests; the resulting features here are `bill_amt4`, `bill_amt5`, and `bill_amt6`, which are likely to be irrelevant, or not related to the target:

```
In [14]:  pd.Series(numerical_features).loc[num_selector.pvalues_>0.05]

Out[14]:  5    bill_amt4
          6    bill_amt5
          7    bill_amt6
          dtype: object
```

We have three candidates for elimination which can be eliminated or can be applied. We have used the second technique in the preceding steps and now we will use the third one in the following section.

The RFE is the third technique in which we will use the `RandomForestClassifier` model, and remember that we have 25 features here:

```
In [15]:  print("Number of featues:", X.shape[1])

          Number of featues: 25
```

So, let's assume that we want to select only 12 features and we want a model that uses only 12 features. So, we are using about half of the features. We can use the RFE object present in `scikit-learn` from the `feature_selection` module. We can use this to actually select these 12 features using the RFE technique. So, we instantiate this object by passing the required estimator and the number of features to select:

```
In [16]:  from sklearn.feature_selection import RFE

In [17]:  RF = RandomForestClassifier(n_estimators=100, max_depth=20, max_features='auto',
                                      random_state=55, n_jobs=-1)

In [18]:  recursive_selector = RFE(estimator=RF, n_features_to_select=12)
```

Now, remember that random forest provides us with a metric of feature importance, which can be used with the RFE technique:

```
In [19]:  recursive_selector = recursive_selector.fit(X, y)
```

After using the `fit()` method on the whole dataset, we get `recursive_selector.support_` and `True` for the features that are included in our model, the 12 that we wanted, and we get `False` for the ones that should be eliminated:

```
In [20]:  recursive_selector.support_

Out[20]:  array([ True,   True,   True, False, False, False, False, False,  True,
                  True,   True,   True,  True,  True,  True,  True,  True, False,
                 False, False, False, False, False, False, False], dtype=bool)
```

So, according to this object and method, we should include the 12 most important features in our random forest model in order to predict targets such as limit_bal, age, pay; all of the bill amounts; and pay_amt1, pay_amt2, and pay_amt3, as shown in the following screenshot:

```
In [21]:  print('12 most important features:')
          for x in feature_names[recursive_selector.support_]:
              print(x)

          12 most important features:
          limit_bal
          age
          pay_1
          bill_amt1
          bill_amt2
          bill_amt3
          bill_amt4
          bill_amt5
          bill_amt6
          pay_amt1
          pay_amt2
          pay_amt3
```

These are the features that should be eliminated because they are not very relevant according to this method and this model for predicting the target:

```
In [22]:  print('Features to eliminate:')
          for x in feature_names[~recursive_selector.support_]:
              print(x)

          Features to eliminate:
          pay_2
          pay_3
          pay_4
          pay_5
          pay_6
          pay_amt4
          pay_amt5
          pay_amt6
          grad_school
          university
          high_school
          male
          married
```

Now we can evaluate the simpler model, the one with the 12 features against the full model that we have been using so far, after which we can calculate the metrics using cross-validation. So, in this example, we are using 10-fold cross-validation to get an estimation of the performance of these two models. Remember, this selector model is the full model according to the RFE technique and these are the results:

```
In [23]:  selector_model = cross_validate(estimator=RF,X=X[:,recursive_selector.support_], y=y,
                            scoring=['recall','accuracy'], cv=10, n_jobs=-1)

          full_model = cross_validate(estimator=RF,X=X,y=y,
                            scoring=['recall','accuracy'], cv=10, n_jobs=-1)

In [24]:  metrics = pd.DataFrame({'Full Model Recall':full_model['test_recall'],
                            'Full Model Accuracy':full_model['test_accuracy'],
                            'Selector Model Recall': selector_model['test_recall'],
                            'Selector Model Accuracy': selector_model['test_accuracy']})
```

The full model has a recall of 0.361365, and the model that includes only 12 features has a recall of 0.355791. Since this model has less recall, the full model remains the best one. But if we use half of the features, the full model will also give us similar performance:

```
In [25]:  metrics[['Full Model Recall','Selector Model Recall']].mean()

Out[25]:  Full Model Recall       0.361365
          Selector Model Recall   0.355791
          dtype: float64
```

As you can see in the following screenshot, the values are really close:

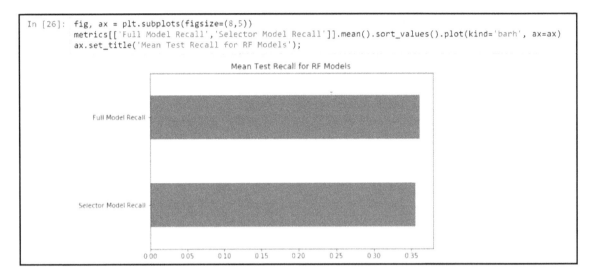

Now you can decide whether you want to use the full model or you want to use the simpler model. This is up to you, but in terms of accuracy we get almost the same, although with still a little bit more accuracy for the full model:

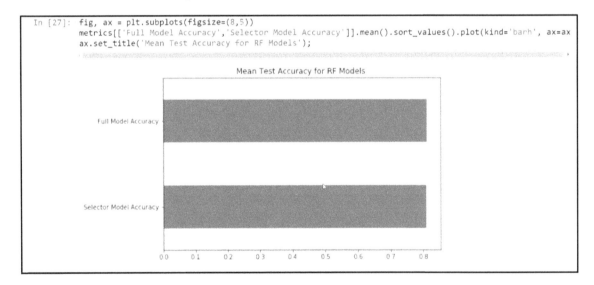

Now, you have a technique to decide whether you want to use a more complicated model that uses more features, or a simpler model.

Dimensionality reduction and PCA

The dimensionality reduction method is the process of reducing the number of features under consideration by obtaining a set of principal variables. The **Principal Component Analysis (PCA)** technique is the most important technique used for dimensionality reduction. Here, we will talk about why we need dimensionality reduction, and we will also see how to perform the PCA technique in `scikit-learn`.

These are the reasons for having a high number of features while working on predictive analytics:

- It enables the simplification of models, in order to make them easier to understand and to interpret. There might be some computational considerations if you are dealing with thousands of features. It might be a good idea to reduce the number of features in order to save computational resources.
- Another reason is to avoid the "curse of dimensionality." Now, this is a technical term and a set of problems that arise when you are working with high-dimensional data.
- This also helps us to minimize overfitting because if you are including a lot of irrelevant features to predict the target, then your model can overfit to that noise. So, removing irrelevant features will help you with overfitting.

Feature selection, seen earlier in this chapter, can be considered a form of dimensionality reduction. When you have a set of features that are closely related or even redundant, PCA will be the preferred technique to encode the same information using less features. So, what is PCA? It's a statistical procedure that converts a set of observations of possibly correlated variables into a set of linearly uncorrelated variables called **principal components**. Let's not go into the mathematical details about what's going on with PCA.

Let's assume we have a dataset that is two-dimensional. PCA identifies a direction where the dataset varies the most and encodes the maximum amount of information on these two features into one single feature to reduce the dimensions from two to one. This method projects every point onto these axes or new dimensions.

As you can see in the following screenshot, the first principal component of these two features would be the projections of the points onto the red line, which is the main mathematical intuition behind what's going on in PCA:

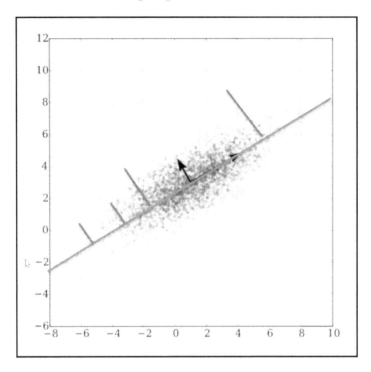

Now, let's go to the Jupyter Notebook to see how to implement the dimensionality reduction method and to apply PCA on the given dataset:

```
In [1]:  import numpy as np
         import matplotlib.pyplot as plt
         import pandas as pd
         import seaborn as sns
         sns.set_style('whitegrid')
         %matplotlib inline
```

In this case, we will use the credit card default dataset. So, here we are doing the transformations that we have covered so far:

```
In [2]: default = pd.read_csv('../data/credit_card_default.csv', index_col="ID")
        default.rename(columns=lambda x: x.lower(), inplace=True)
        default.rename(columns={'pay_0':'pay_1','default payment next month':'default'}, inplace=True)
        # Base values: female, other_education, not_married
        default['grad_school'] = (default['education'] == 1).astype('int')
        default['university'] = (default['education'] == 2).astype('int')
        default['high_school'] = (default['education'] == 3).astype('int')
        default.drop('education', axis=1, inplace=True)

        default['male'] = (default['sex']==1).astype('int')
        default.drop('sex', axis=1, inplace=True)

        default['married'] = (default['marriage'] == 1).astype('int')
        default.drop('marriage', axis=1, inplace=True)

        # For pay_n features if >0 then it means the customer was delayed on that month
        pay_features = ['pay_' + str(i) for i in range(1,7)]
        for p in pay_features:
            default[p] = (default[p] > 0).astype(int)
```

Now, let's take a look at the bill amount features. We have six of these features, the history of the bill amounts from one to six months ago, which are closely related, as you can see from the visualization generated from the following screenshot of code snippets:

```
In [3]: bill_amt_features = ['bill_amt'+str(i) for i in range(1,7)]
        sns.pairplot(default, vars=bill_amt_features, hue='default',
                plot_kws={'s':2});
```

So, they represent the same information. If you see a customer with a very high bill amount two or three months ago, it is very likely that they also got a very high bill amount one month ago. So, these features, as you can see from the visualization shown in the following screenshot, are really closely related:

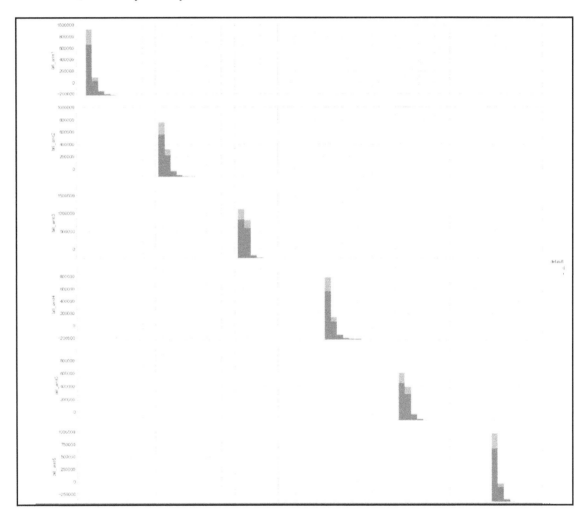

We confirm this with the calculation of the correlation coefficient. As you can see, they are really highly correlated:

```
In [4]:  default[bill_amt_features].corr()
Out[4]:
```

	bill_amt1	bill_amt2	bill_amt3	bill_amt4	bill_amt5	bill_amt6
bill_amt1	1.000000	0.951484	0.892279	0.860272	0.829779	0.802650
bill_amt2	0.951484	1.000000	0.928326	0.892482	0.859778	0.831594
bill_amt3	0.892279	0.928326	1.000000	0.923969	0.883910	0.853320
bill_amt4	0.860272	0.892482	0.923969	1.000000	0.940134	0.900941
bill_amt5	0.829779	0.859778	0.883910	0.940134	1.000000	0.946197
bill_amt6	0.802650	0.831594	0.853320	0.900941	0.946197	1.000000

The correlation between the bill amount one month ago and two months ago is `0.95`. We have very high correlations, which is a good opportunity to apply a dimensionality reduction technique, such as PCA in `scikit-learn`, for which we import it from `sklearn.decomposition`, as shown in the following screenshot:

```
In [5]:  from sklearn.decomposition import PCA
```

After that, we instantiate this `PCA` object. Then, we pass the columns or the features that we want to apply PCA decomposition to:

```
In [6]:  bill_amt_pca = PCA()
         bill_amt_pca.fit(default[bill_amt_features])
Out[6]:  PCA(copy=True, iterated_power='auto', n_components=None, random_state=None,
             svd_solver='auto', tol=0.0, whiten=False)
```

So after using the `fit()` method derived from this object, we receive one of the attributes, the explained variance ratio, as shown in the following screenshot:

```
In [7]:  explainded_variance= pd.Series(100*bill_amt_pca.explained_variance_ratio_,
                                index=['bill_amt_comp_'+str(i) for i in range(1,7)])
```

Let's plot this quantity to get a feel for what's going on with these features. As you can see here, we get the explained variance of all six components:

```
In [8]:  fig, ax = plt.subplots(figsize=(8,5))
         explainded_variance.plot(kind='barh', ax=ax);
         ax.set_title('Explained Variance, PCA of Bill Amount Features');
```

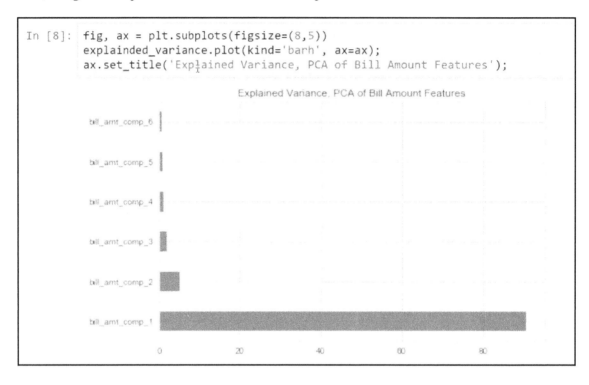

The way to read this plot is that the first component of the PCA that we did on these six features encodes more than 90% of the total variance of all six features. The second one shows a very small variance, and the third, fourth, fifth, and sixth components also have minimal variance.

Now, we can see this in the plot of cumulative explained variance shown in the following screenshot:

```
In [9]:  fig, ax = plt.subplots(figsize=(8,5))
         explainded_variance.cumsum().plot()
         ax.set_title('Cumulative Explained Variance, PCA of Bill Amount Features');
```

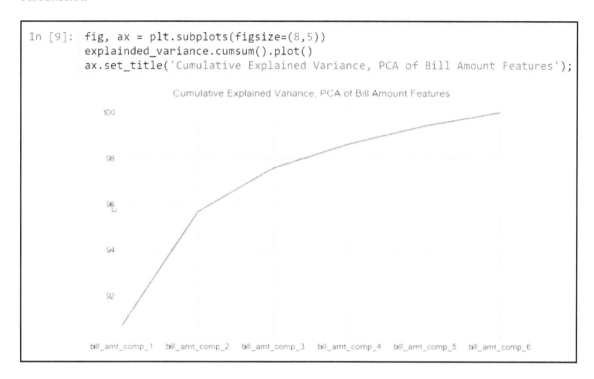

As you can see, the first component encodes more than 90% of the variance of the six features that we used. So, you are getting more than 90% of the information in just one feature. Therefore, instead of using six features, you can use just one single feature and still get more than 90% of the variance. Or, you can use the first two components and get more than 95% of the total information contained in the six features in just two features, the first and second components of this PCA. So, this is how this works in practice and we can use this as one technique for performing feature engineering.

Feature engineering

Feature engineering plays a vital role in making machine learning algorithms work and, if carried out properly, it enhances the predictive ability of machine learning algorithms. In other words, feature engineering is the process of extracting existing features or creating new features from the raw data using domain knowledge, the context of the problem, or specialized techniques that result in more accurate predictive models. This is an activity where domain knowledge and creativity play a very important role. This is an important process, which can significantly improve the performance of our predictive models. The more context you have about a problem, the better your ability to create new and useful features. Basically, the feature engineering process converts the features into input values that algorithms can understand.

There are various ways of implementing feature engineering. You might not find all of the techniques feasible and may end up excluding a few. The motive here is not to have an academic discussion about this topic, but to show you some of the common things that we do when we work with features and when we try to create new features. The first one is scaling features, used to transform their range to a more suitable one. The other one is to encode information in a better way, and we will see an example of this later in this chapter. Feature engineering involves creating new features from existing ones so that you can combine existing features by performing some mathematical operations on them. Another way of creating new features is by using a dimensionality reduction technique, such as PCA, which we saw previously. It doesn't matter what technique you use, as long as you make it creative. As mentioned previously, the more knowledge you have about the problem, the better.

Creating new features

We will be using the credit card default and diamond datasets here. Now, let's go to the Jupyter Notebook to create new features and see what these techniques are in practice:

```
In [1]:  import numpy as np
         import matplotlib.pyplot as plt
         import pandas as pd
         import seaborn as sns
         sns.set_style('whitegrid')
         %matplotlib inline
```

Let's import the credit card default dataset by executing a few commands, as shown in the following screenshot:

```
In [2]:  default = pd.read_csv('../data/credit_card_default.csv', index_col="ID")
         default.rename(columns=lambda x: x.lower(), inplace=True)
         default.rename(columns={'pay_0':'pay_1','default payment next month':'default'}, inplace=True)

         default['male'] = (default['sex']==1).astype('int')
         default.drop('sex', axis=1, inplace=True)

         default['married'] = (default['marriage'] == 1).astype('int')
         default.drop('marriage', axis=1, inplace=True)

         # For pay_n features if >0 then it means the customer was delayed on that month
         pay_features = ['pay_' + str(i) for i in range(1,7)]
         for p in pay_features:
             default[p] = (default[p] > 0).astype(int)
```

The first transformation that we will do is to create another way to encode the information that we have in the education feature. So far, we have been using one encoding technique in the education feature, and we will use the context of the x variable to come up with another encoding. People with graduate-level education are more highly educated than people with other levels of education. So, we can come up with some sort of points system for these features; for example, we can assign two points for people with graduate-level education, maybe one point for people with university-level education, and negative points for the other levels of education that we have in this dataset.
Let's take a look at the following screenshot to see how this is done:

```
In [3]:  def transform_education(x):
             if x==1: # 1==graduate school, give it a 2
                 return 2
             elif x==2: # 2==university, give it a 1
                 return 1
             else:
                 return -1 # give a negative value to all other levels of education

         default['education'] = default['education'].apply(transform_education)
```

The previous screenshot reflects the sequence that we have in these education levels, so this could be an another way to encode information. This might or might not be helpful in predicting defaulters for the next month. However, we can try this new technique to encode this information and see the results in the following screenshot:

```
In [4]:  default.groupby(['married','male'])['default'].mean().unstack()

Out[4]:
                male        0        1

          married

                0   0.197345  0.227979

                1   0.219625  0.259345
```

Another technique that we can use in this dataset is to use the bill amount and payment amount features in the context of this problem to calculate the difference between these two variables/features. So, if we take the bill amount from a particular month and subtract the payment amount for that month, we will get an amount or quantity. In this example, we are calling the `bill_minus_pay` variable, which represents the payment made by the client against the bill for that month. So, this newly derived quantity can be used to predict defaulters for the next month. We have included them in a potential predictive model for this dataset:

```
In [4]:  for i in range(1,7):
             i = str(i)
             new_var_name = 'bill_minus_pay' + i
             default[new_var_name] = default['bill_amt'+i] - default['pay_amt'+i]

In [5]:  bill_minus_pay_features = ['bill_minus_pay'+str(i) for i in range(1,7)]
         default[bill_minus_pay_features].hist(figsize=(11,5), layout=(2,3), bins=30);
```

Let's now take a look at the following output, which depicts the defaulters for a particular month:

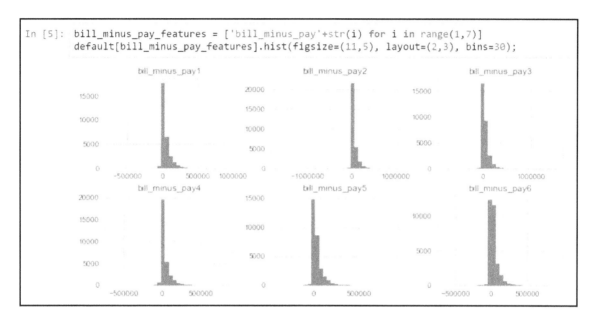

```
In [5]:  bill_minus_pay_features = ['bill_minus_pay'+str(i) for i in range(1,7)]
         default[bill_minus_pay_features].hist(figsize=(11,5), layout=(2,3), bins=30);
```

Another method that we can use here, now that we have part of the information of these features in a new feature called `bill_minus_pay`, is that we can summarize the main information of the six features shown in the preceding screenshot in just one feature using the PCA technique:

We can do the same operation with the pay features. From the previous analysis, we know that the `pay_1` feature is very important for predicting who is going to pay next. So, in order to reduce the other five `pay_i` features to just two, we are reducing the six bill amount features to just one, and the six `pay_i` features to two. Apart from this, we again apply the PCA technique on the remaining five `pay_i` features to reduce these five to just one. Take a look at the following screenshot:

```
In [8]:  pay_features = ['pay_'+str(i) for i in range(2,7)]
         pay_features_pca = PCA().fit(default[pay_features])
         pay_features_pca.explained_variance_ratio_

Out[8]:  array([ 0.62640566,  0.15478995,  0.10049793,  0.07279835,  0.04550811])

In [9]:  pay_features_pca = PCA(n_components=2).fit_transform(default[pay_features])
         default['new_pay1'] = pay_features_pca[:,0]
         default['new_pay2'] = pay_features_pca[:,1]
```

These are some of the feature engineering techniques, with examples, that you can perform on your datasets, but you might want to create other transformations or variables from the existing ones.

Now, let's see a couple of examples in the diamonds dataset. We need to import the diamonds dataset by executing a few commands, as shown in the following screenshot:

As seen in the preceding screenshot, we have transformed some of the categorical features using the encoding technique. Now, let's take a look at our imported dataset, shown in the following screenshot:

```
In [11]:  diamonds.head()
```

Out[11]:

	carat	depth	table	price	x	y	z	cut_Good	cut_Ideal	cut_Premium	...	color_H	color_I	color_J	clarity_IF
0	0.23	61.5	55.0	326	3.95	3.98	2.43	0	1	0	...	0	0	0	0
1	0.21	59.8	61.0	326	3.89	3.84	2.31	0	0	1	...	0	0	0	0
2	0.23	56.9	65.0	327	4.05	4.07	2.31	1	0	0	...	0	0	0	0
3	0.29	62.4	58.0	334	4.20	4.23	2.63	0	0	1	...	0	1	0	0
4	0.31	63.3	58.0	335	4.34	4.35	2.75	1	0	0	...	0	0	1	0

5 rows × 24 columns

This is what our scatter plot matrix with four features, x, y, z, and `price`, looks like. The first three features refer to the measurements of the diamond, and `price` represents how those three features are related to the pricing of the diamond:

```
In [12]:  sns.pairplot(diamonds[['x','y','z','price']], plot_kws={'s':2});
```

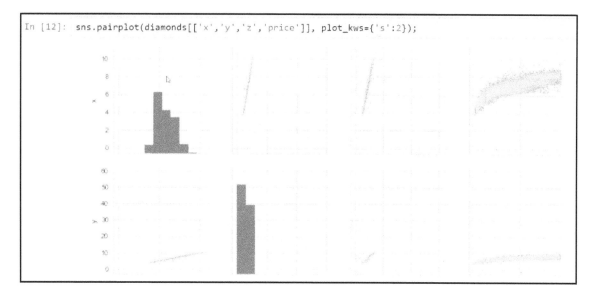

In the preceding screenshot, as you can see, there is a very strong linear relationship between the first three features, which is one of the interesting things in this scatter plot matrix.

As diamonds are three-dimensional objects, we will combine these three features into just a single feature, called volume.

Now, we will multiply the measurements of the x, y, and z axes, which will derive a number that is close to the volume of that object:

```
In [13]: diamonds['volume'] = diamonds['x']*diamonds['y']*diamonds['z']
```

Now, we know that they are not boxes, and they don't have any fixed shape. However, this will be a really good approximation of the volume of the diamonds. So, this can be another way in which we can create a new feature volume from the existing features in this dataset.

In the next screenshot, we have the volume of our object and also the weight of the diamond, which is measured as carat, and we will use these to create a new feature called density:

```
In [15]: diamonds['density'] = diamonds['carat']/diamonds['volume']
```

As you can see in the preceding screenshot, we have divided the carat by the volume in order to get the density of the diamond object.

This is how we created two features from the given context, which justifies the statement: "the more the knowledge or context of the problem, the better". As you can see, with just the provided knowledge of the problem, we were able to come up with new features.

Now, let's try and see how helpful these features might be in predicting models. The example we will use here is, how you can combine existing features to produce new features. The following plot shows the close relationship between the volume and price:

```
In [15]:  diamonds[diamonds['volume']<600].plot.scatter(x='volume', y='price', s=1, alpha=0.1);
```

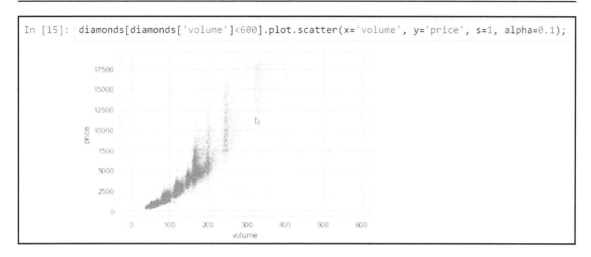

We can assume that the volume will be helpful in predicting the price.

However, in the following scatterplot of density and price, we see that all diamonds have the same expected density:

```
In [20]:  fig, ax = plt.subplots(figsize=(8,5))
          diamonds.plot.scatter(x='density', y='price', s=2, alpha=0.1, ax=ax)
          ax.set_xlim(0,0.015);
```

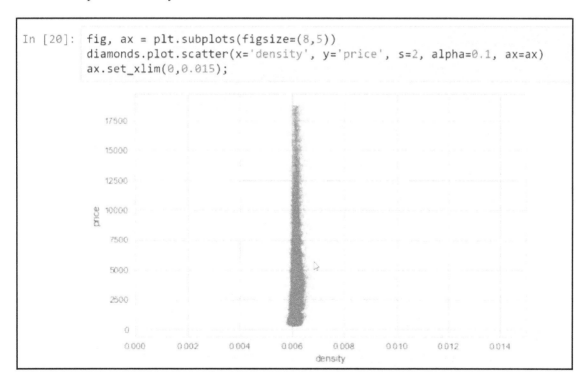

When we see the correlation between `price` and `carat`, which we already had, it seems that `density` might not relate to `price` much:

```
In [16]:  diamonds[['price','carat','volume','density']].corr()
Out[16]:

                    price       carat      volume      density

         price    1.000000    0.921591    0.902385    0.143440

         carat    0.921591    1.000000    0.976308    0.206805

        volume    0.902385    0.976308    1.000000    0.128187

       density    0.143440    0.206805    0.128187    1.000000
```

So, this new feature might not help much in prediction. The volume and carat features have the same kind of relationship. We might not gain a lot of predictive power with this feature, but the main goal behind explaining this example was to show how to combine different features that you already have in your dataset to create new features.

This is what feature engineering is all about. You might also come up with other features for this dataset.

Improving models with feature engineering

Now that we have seen how feature engineering techniques help in building predictive models, let's try and improve the performance of these models and evaluate whether the newly built model works better than the previous built model. Then, we will talk about two very important concepts that you must always keep in mind when doing predictive analytics, and these are the reducible and irreducible errors in your predictive models.

Let's first import the necessary modules, as shown in the following screenshot:

```
In [1]:  import numpy as np
         import matplotlib.pyplot as plt
         import pandas as pd

         from sklearn.ensemble import RandomForestClassifier
         from sklearn.model_selection import GridSearchCV
         from sklearn.preprocessing import RobustScaler
         from sklearn.model_selection import train_test_split
         from sklearn.decomposition import PCA
         from sklearn.metrics import accuracy_score, recall_score, precision_score

         %matplotlib inline
```

So, let's go to the Jupyter Notebook and take a look at the imported credit card default dataset that we saw earlier in this chapter, but as you can see, some modifications have been made to this dataset:

```
In [2]:  default = pd.read_csv('../data/credit_card_default.csv', index_col="ID")
         default.rename(columns=lambda x: x.lower(), inplace=True)
         default.rename(columns={'pay_0':'pay_1','default payment next month':'default'}, inplace=True)

         default['grad_school'] = (default['education'] == 1).astype(int)
         default['university'] = (default['education'] == 2).astype(int)
         default['high_school'] = (default['education'] == 3).astype(int)
         default.drop('education', axis=1, inplace=True)

         default['married_male'] = ((default['sex']==1) & (default['marriage'] == 1)).astype(int)
         default['not_married_female'] = ((default['sex']==2) & (default['marriage'] != 1)).astype(int)
         default.drop(['sex','marriage'], axis=1, inplace=True)

         # For pay_n features if >0 then it means the customer was delayed on that month
         pay_features = ['pay_' + str(i) for i in range(1,7)]
         for p in pay_features:
             default[p] = (default[p] > 0).astype(int)
```

For this model, instead of transforming the `sex` and `marriage` features into two dummy features, the ones that we have been using were `male` and `married`; therefore, let's encode the information in a slightly different way to see if this works better. So, we will encode the information as `married_male` and `not_married_female`, and see if this works better. This is the first transformation that we are doing here. This is what the dataset looks like:

```
In [3]:  default.head()
Out[3]:
```

ID	limit_bal	age	pay_1	pay_2	pay_3	pay_4	pay_5	pay_6	bill_amt1	bill_amt2	...	pay_amt3	pay_amt4	pay_amt5
1	20000	24	1	1	0	0	0	0	3913	3102	...	0	0	0
2	120000	26	0	1	0	0	0	1	2682	1725	...	1000	1000	0
3	90000	34	0	0	0	0	0	0	29239	14027	...	1000	1000	1000
4	50000	37	0	0	0	0	0	0	46990	48233	...	1200	1100	1069
5	50000	57	0	0	0	0	0	0	8617	5670	...	10000	9000	689

5 rows × 26 columns

Now, let's do a little bit more feature engineering. The first thing that we will do is calculate these new features, which are built from subtracting the payment amount from the bill amount, as shown in the following screenshot:

```
In [4]:  # Bill amount minus payment
         for i in range(1,7):
             i = str(i)
             new_var_name = 'bill_minus_pay' + i
             default[new_var_name] = default['bill_amt'+i] - default['pay_amt'+i]

         # Reducing the 6 bill amount features to 1
         bill_amt_features = ['bill_amt'+str(i) for i in range(1,7)]
         bill_amt_pca = PCA(n_components=1)
         default['bill_amt_new_feat'] = bill_amt_pca.fit_transform(default[bill_amt_features])[:,0]
         default.drop(bill_amt_features, axis=1, inplace=True)

         # Reducing the 5 pay_i features to 2
         pay_features = ['pay_'+str(i) for i in range(2,7)]
         pay_features_pca = PCA(n_components=2).fit_transform(default[pay_features])
         default['new_pay1'] = pay_features_pca[:,0]
         default['new_pay2'] = pay_features_pca[:,1]
         default.drop(pay_features, axis=1, inplace=True)
```

For this problem, we will perform one mathematical operation. We will use the new features shown in the preceding screenshot to predict the target. Most of the information in the bill amount features is now encoded in these features, which are not needed anymore, but instead of throwing them away, what we can do is reduce the six bill amount features to just one using the PCA technique. So, let's apply the PCA technique to reduce the six features to just one component. Now there is a new feature called `bill_amt_new_feat`. So, this was the second feature engineering step that we performed. Finally, for the `pay_i` features, we will preserve the first one as is, and apply the PCA technique to the last five features, `pay_2`, `pay_3`, `pay_4`, `pay_5`, and `pay_6`, to reduce these five features to just two components. You can use the `fit_transform` method on the `PCA` object to get the components.

Now, let's take a look at the following screenshot, showing all of the features that have to do with money. As you can see, the variances here are really huge because the currency amounts are large:

```
In [5]: money_features = ['limit_bal', 'pay_amt1', 'pay_amt2', 'pay_amt3', 'pay_amt4', 'pay_amt5', 'pay_amt6',
                          'bill_minus_pay1', 'bill_minus_pay2', 'bill_minus_pay3', 'bill_minus_pay4',
                          'bill_minus_pay5', 'bill_minus_pay6', 'bill_amt_new_feat']

In [6]: default[money_features].var()

Out[6]: limit_bal          1.683446e+10
        pay_amt1           2.743423e+08
        pay_amt2           5.308817e+08
        pay_amt3           3.100051e+08
        pay_amt4           2.454286e+08
        pay_amt5           2.334266e+08
        pay_amt6           3.160383e+08
        bill_minus_pay1    5.354403e+09
        bill_minus_pay2    5.265815e+09
        bill_minus_pay3    4.801847e+09
        bill_minus_pay4    4.121718e+09
        bill_minus_pay5    3.666711e+09
        bill_minus_pay6    3.618178e+09
        bill_amt_new_feat  2.418877e+10
        dtype: float64
```

Now, rescale these features by dividing them by 1,000 in order to reduce the variances, as shown in the following screenshot:

```
In [7]:  default[money_features] = default[money_features]/1000

In [8]:  default[money_features].var()

Out[8]:  limit_bal              16834.455682
         pay_amt1                 274.342256
         pay_amt2                 530.881709
         pay_amt3                 310.005092
         pay_amt4                 245.428561
         pay_amt5                 233.426624
         pay_amt6                 316.038289
         bill_minus_pay1         5354.403462
         bill_minus_pay2         5265.815238
         bill_minus_pay3         4801.847004
         bill_minus_pay4         4121.718431
         bill_minus_pay5         3666.710625
         bill_minus_pay6         3618.177789
         bill_amt_new_feat      24188.771200
         dtype: float64
```

This helps us to make these numbers understandable. So, this is the other transformation that we did, and now let's train our model with these new features.

Training your model

The following model is a new module, as it has different features compared to the other models. Since the features have changed, we need to find the best hyperparameters for the RandomForestClassifier module using the GridSearchCV module. So, perhaps the previously found best parameters are not the best for these new features; therefore, we will run the GridSearchCV algorithm again:

```
In [10]:  parameter_grid = {'n_estimators': [25,50,100],
                             'max_depth': [15,20,30],
                             'max_features': ['auto','sqrt']}

          RF_classifier = GridSearchCV(RandomForestClassifier(random_state=12),
                                param_grid=parameter_grid, refit=True,
                                scoring='recall', cv=10, n_jobs=-1)

          RF_classifier.fit(X_train, y_train)
          y_pred_test = RF_classifier.predict(X_test)
          test_accuracy = accuracy_score(y_pred=y_pred_test, y_true=y_test)
          test_recall = recall_score(y_pred=y_pred_test, y_true=y_test)
          print('Test Accuracy:', test_accuracy)
          print('Test Recall:', test_recall)

          Test Accuracy: 0.802
          Test Recall: 0.329819277108
```

As shown in the following screenshot, in this case the best combination of parameters for these new features is max _depth of 30, max_features in auto, and n_estimators (number of estimators) should be 100:

```
In [11]:  RF_classifier.best_params_

Out[11]:  {'max_depth': 30, 'max_features': 'auto', 'n_estimators': 100}
```

Now, let's evaluate this new model that we have built using feature engineering, and let's compare it with the previous metrics that we have from the previously built model:

```
In [12]:  y_pred_proba = RF_classifier.predict_proba(X_test)[:,1]
          y_pred_test = (y_pred_proba >= 0.2).astype('int')
          print("Recall: ", 100*round(recall_score(y_pred=y_pred_test, y_true=y_test),4))
          print("Precision: ", 100*round(precision_score(y_pred=y_pred_test, y_true=y_test),4))

          Recall:  71.39
          Precision:  37.38

          for the first model we had:

            • Recall: 68.9
            • Precision: 37.9
```

As you can see in the preceding screenshot, we are using a threshold of 0.2. This model generates a recall of 71.39% and a precision of 37.38. Here, the precisions are similar, but, as mentioned earlier, the recall might be the metric that we should care about, as it's slightly different compared to the previous one. We got a little better recall for this model; the change may only be 2% or 3%, which might not look like much, but remember that in these financial applications, an improvement of 1% or 2% could, in practice, mean a lot of money. So, we got a slight improvement in the predictive power of our model using this little feature engineering technique; let's take a look at the feature importance in the following screenshot:

```
In [13]:  fig, ax = plt.subplots(figsize=(8,6))
          feature_importances = pd.Series(data=RF_classifier.best_estimator_.feature_importances_, index=feature_
          feature_importances.sort_values().plot(kind='barh', ax=ax)
          ax.set_xlabel('Importance')
          ax.set_ylabel('Feature')
          ax.set_title('Feature importances from Random Forest model')
          ax.grid();
```

You can assess whether this feature importance make sense in the following screenshot of the random forest model:

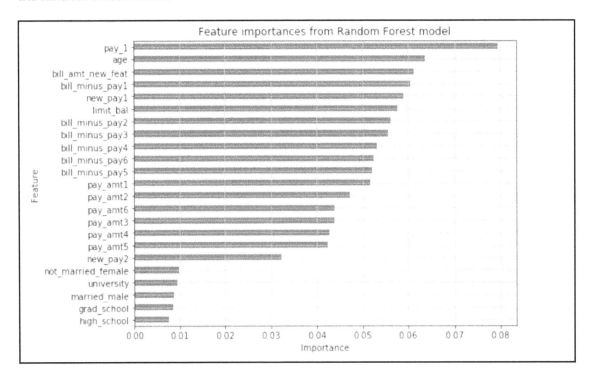

You can compare this feature importance with the previous ones. There are a lot of things that you can do after you have applied feature engineering. We may improve performance and gain insight from the model. It's been observed that we improved our model a little bit by using this technique. Now, you can come up with different ways to combine the existing features to improve the model even more. This was just a small, simple example to show you that you can actually play around with the features in a way that actually makes sense.

Reducible and irreducible error

Before moving on, there are two really important concepts to be covered for predictive analytics. Errors can be divided into the following two types:

- **Reducible errors**: These errors can be reduced by making certain improvements to the model
- **Irreducible errors**: These errors cannot be reduced at all

Let's assume that, in machine learning, there is a relationship between features and target that is represented with a function, as shown in the following screenshot:

$$y = f(X) + \epsilon$$

Let's assume that the target (**y**) is the underlying supposition of machine learning, and the relationship between the features and the target is given by a function. Since, in most cases we consider that there is some randomness in the relationship between features and target, we add a noise term here, which will always be present in reality. This is the underlying supposition in machine learning.

In models, we try to approximate the theoretical function by using an actual function while performing feature engineering, tuning the parameters, and so on:

$$y_{pred} = \hat{f}(X)$$

So, our predictions are the results of the application of these approximations to the conceptual or theoretical **f**. All that we do in machine learning is try to approximate this **f** function by training the model.

Training a model means approximating this function. It is possible to show mathematically that the expected error, defined as the difference between the real **y** and the predicted **y**, can be decomposed into two terms. One term is called **Reducible error** and the other one is called **Irreducible error**, as shown in the following screenshot:

$$ExpectedError = E(y - y_{pred}) = [\hat{f}(X) - f(X)]^2 + Var[\epsilon]$$

Reducible error   **Irreducible error**

Now, the **Irreducible error** term is the variance of this random term. You don't have any control over this term. There will always be an irreducible error component. So, your model will always make mistakes; it doesn't matter how many features and data points you have, your model cannot always be 100% correct. What we must try to do is to use better and more sophisticated methods to perform feature engineering, and try to approximate our estimation to the real function. Just because you are working with more sophisticated models or you have more data, your model will not be perfect and you will not be able to predict exactly what **y** is, because there is some randomness in almost all the processes that you will work with. So this is the end of a very interesting section.

Summary

In this chapter, we talked about feature selection methods, how to distinguish between useful features, and features that are not likely to be helpful in prediction. We talked about dimensionality reduction and we learned how to perform PCA in `scikit-learn`. We also talked about feature engineering, and we tried to come up with new features in the datasets that we have been using so far. Finally, we tried to improve our credit card model by coming up with new features, and by working with all of the techniques that we learned in this chapter. I hope you have enjoyed this chapter.

In the next chapter, we will learn about artificial neural networks and how the `tensorflow` library is used when working with neural networks and artificial intelligence.

4
Introduction to Artificial Neural Networks and TensorFlow

In this chapter, we will give an introduction to **artificial neural networks** (**ANNs**), which are basically computational models inspired by living brains, and perceptrons, which are the building blocks for ANNs. We will also talk about all of the elements to consider when building a deep neural network model. Then, we will talk about TensorFlow, which is the library that we will use to create these deep neural network models. Finally, we will talk about the core concepts that we need to understand about TensorFlow in order to use these library concepts, such as variables, placeholders, sessions, graphs, and others that are essential for using this library.

The following are the topics that will be covered as we progress:

- Introduction to ANNs
- Elements of a deep neural network
- Installation of and introduction to TensorFlow
- Core concepts in TensorFlow

Introduction to ANNs

ANNs are biologically inspired computational models that can be used to train a computer to perform a task using data. These models are part of the broad category of machine learning models. The distinction between these models and others is that these models are based on a collection of connected units called **artificial neurons**.

There are many types of ANNs and, in this book, we will use one specific type, which is called the **multilayer perceptron** (**MLP**). Please note that there are a lot more variations of ANNs. These are machine learning models and we can use them for classification and regression tasks, but we can actually extend these models and apply them to other very specific tasks such as computer vision, speech recognition, and machine translation. These models are the basis of the exciting and growing field of deep learning, which has been really successful in the last few years in many areas.

Perceptrons

Perceptrons are the simplest type of artificial neuron, invented as a simple model for binary classification. Let's use the context of the dataset that we have been using in this book, the credit card dataset. Let's say that we have only two features for classifying defaulters and nondefaulters: age and bill amount. So the idea of the perceptron is to create some kind of a score. To do so, you take one constant, w1 ,and multiply it by the value of age, and then you add another constant, w2, which is multiplied by the value of the bill amount as follows:

```
score = w1age+w2bill
```

As a rule, we classify this person as a defaulter if score > b.

So, from this simple operation, we create a score. Then, we follow the rule to classify people as defaulters or as nondefaulters. So, if this score is greater than some number, then we classify this person as a defaulter.

An equivalent way to state this rule is shown in the following screenshot:

$$y\_pred = \begin{cases} 1 \ if \ (w_1 age + w_2 bill - b) > 0 \\ 0 \ if \ (w_1 age + w_2 bill - b) \leq 0 \end{cases}$$

So, the prediction of this model will be 1, or defaulter, if the quantity is greater than 0, and the prediction will be 0, or nondefaulter, if this quantity is less than or equal to 0. The b value is also known as the threshold or bias.

In general, if we have n features, then our perceptron would look similar to the following screenshot:

$$y\_pred = \begin{cases} 1 \; if \; \sum_{j=1}^{n} w_j x_j - b > 0 \\ 0 \; if \; \sum_{j=1}^{n} w_j x_j - b \leq 0 \end{cases}$$

As you can see, we have the same form. We predict **1** if the sum of the weights times the values of our features **-b** is actually greater than **0**, otherwise, we predict **0**. Assuming that all features are on the same scale, the weights would represent the importance of each feature in making the decision. So, we know that for this particular problem we have, all features are in very different scales. For example, ages are in different scales than bill amount, but let's say that you set all of the features to a similar scale. You can think about the **w** variables as the weights, and they are the most important part of each feature while making the decision.

The following screenshot shows another way to visualize this perceptron:

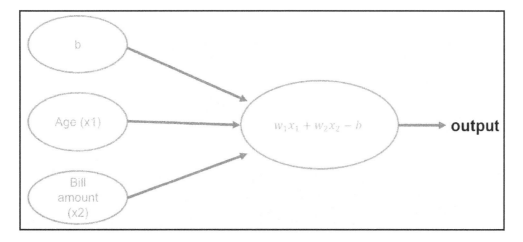

So, you have the values of the threshold or the bias, **b**, and you have the value of **Age, x1** ,and the value of **Bill amount, x2**. So the three values go into an operation, and then you get an output. Now, there is a little modification that we can do to the perceptron, and this is to add what is known as an **activation function**. An activation function is any function that takes the result of the operation and performs some transformation to the input values using the **f** function. So the input for the activation function is the resulting quantity from the operation, and then, after applying activation function **f**, we will get the following output:

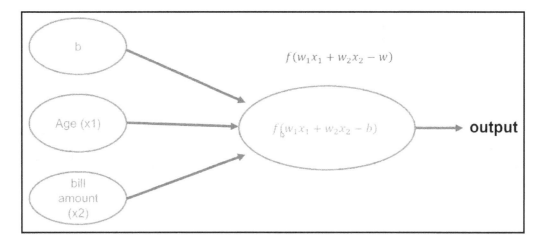

So, this is the perceptron. We can add an activation function to the perceptron and then we get the rule or the classification 1 or 0.

Now, maybe you are wondering how do we decide which are the best weights and threshold for our perceptron? What activation function can we use? The answers to these questions are provided by the perceptron learning algorithm. So, there is a learning algorithm that we can use to actually train perceptrons. The good thing about perceptrons is that they are very simple to understand. However, they are very weak in performance when compared to more sophisticated methods, such as the methods that we used in previous chapters. So, it is not worth actually learning about this perceptron learning algorithm. However, these very simple models are the building blocks for ANNs.

Multilayer perceptron

ANNs are models based on perceptrons or other similar basic building blocks, and the ones that we will learn about in this book are based on perceptrons. One of the most popular ANN models is the MLP, which we will use in this book. The motivation for using perceptrons in an ANN is that, instead of using one single perceptron for classification, what if we used many of them? Take a look at the following screenshot:

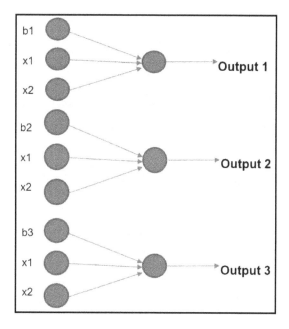

Here, we have three perceptrons and we notice that we have a different bias for each perceptron. But the values for our features will be the same in all cases. If we use three perceptrons, we will get three output values, but we know that this is a binary classification problem so we need only one output. So, now that we have three output values, we can combine them or we can view these output values as input values for another perceptron. Take a look at the following screenshot:

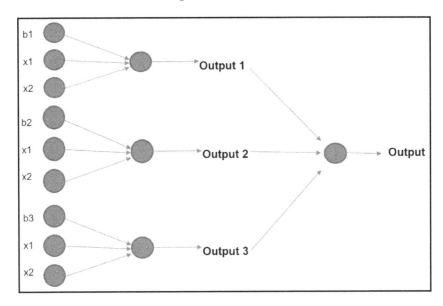

As you can see in the following screenshot, we can take the output values from the preceding perceptrons and fit them as input values to another perceptron, and this perceptron will give us the output. So, this is the intuition on how to build neural networks or MLPs, and this is an example of an ANN:

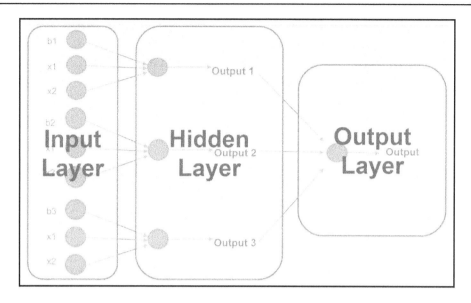

In the preceding screenshot, we have the following three layers of an MLP:

- **Input Layer**: In this layer, you have the original data or the training data that you will use to train this model
- **Hidden Layer**: This middle layer is the output from the preceding perceptron, which is used as the input for the next perceptron
- **Output Layer**: In this layer, you have the output that you get from the network

The following screenshot is another way to visualize the same ANN:

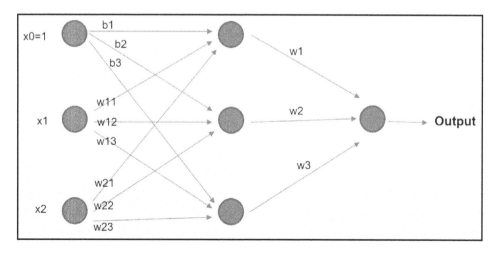

This is a more compact way to visualize it, but it's actually the same network. So, instead of having three biases, we add one constant feature, **1**, for every observation. This value of **1** gets multiplied by the different biases and goes as input to the neurons in our hidden layer. The value of **x1** gets multiplied by some weight and goes as input for the next neurons, and the same happens with the value of **x2**. Then, the result of the neurons in the hidden layer is used as input for the last perceptron in our network, which is the overall output.

Elements of a deep neural network model

The motivation for **deep neural networks** (**DNNs**) is similar, and the question here is, instead of using one single hidden layer, what if we use many hidden layers? So in that case, our model will look similar to the following:

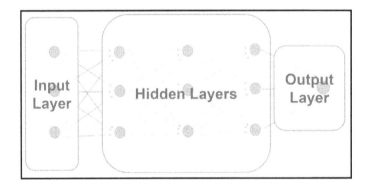

Here, we have the same input layer. However, in this case, we will have many hidden layers and the output layer will stay the same. The key thing here is the hidden part of the network, the hidden layers; instead of having just one, we have many hidden layers and this is called a **DNN**.

Deep learning

Deep learning is a set of machine learning models based on neural networks and the associated techniques to train such models using data. There are many deep learning models. They are a class of machine learning algorithm with the following characteristics:

- These models use a set of many layers of nonlinear processing units, which can perform abstract feature extraction and transformation
- These models use some form of gradient descent for training through backpropagation

- They usually need a lot of data and a lot of computational power for these models to perform very well
- These models are now considered state-of the-art for many applications such as computer vision, speech recognition, and game playing

Elements of an MLP model

There are a lot of things to consider when building a deep learning model in an multilayer perceptron. You have to consider the architecture, the activation function, the optimization algorithm, the `loss` function, the weight initialization strategy, the regularization strategy, and the training strategy. We will discuss more about them in the following list:

- **Architecture**: The first element that you need to consider when building deep learning models is the architecture of your MLP. When we say architecture, we are talking about the number of layers and the number of neurons per layer. The number of neurons in the input layer is determined by the number of features that you have in your dataset. The same thing is true for the number of output values. So, they are basically determined by your problem in a classification setting. The number of output values is usually the number of classes in your classification problem, and in a regression problem you will have only one output in your output layer. The choice that you have to make is how many hidden layers you are going to use and the number of neurons per hidden layer. There are not easy rules to set these numbers; in practice, what we do is we use a few layers at first. If a few layers don't work, maybe we add more layers, and the number of neurons for each layer is a number between the number of input values and the number of outputs, `[n_inputs, n_outputs]`.

> This is just a rule of thumb. However, there are more formal methods to choose the number of hidden layers and the number of neurons, and researchers are constantly trying to come up with better methods for choosing these values.

- **Activation function**: The activation function is the function that is used in every neuron in the hidden layers. There are many choices; **sigmoid** was the first function used when these models were developed, but then researchers found that there are many problems with using this function, so they came up with other activation functions such as the **rectified Linear Unit (ReLU)**, the **hyperbolic tangent**, the **leaky ReLU**, and some other choices that we will use in the examples as we progress.

- **Optimization algorithm**: This is the algorithm that will be used to learn the weights of the networks. Each algorithm that you choose has different hyperparameters that need to be chosen by you, the modeler. The most basic algorithm to train these networks is **gradient descent**. However, gradient descent can be slow and also has some problems, so researchers have come up with other algorithms such as **momentum optimizers**, **AdaGrad**, **RMSProp**, and the **Adam** moment algorithm. In TensorFlow, we have a lot of algorithms that we can choose from, including the Adam moment algorithm, and this is actually the one that we are going to use in the examples.

- **Loss function**: This is the function that will produce the quantity that will be minimized by the optimizer. The choice of loss function depends on the problem. If we are doing a regression problem, you can choose the mean squared error or the mean pairwise squared error. For classification problems, there are more choices such as cross entropy, square loss, and hinge loss. This is similar to trial and error; sometimes, one loss function will work for your problem and sometimes it will not. So, this is why you have to consider a lot of different loss functions. However, keep in mind that the loss function will produce the quantity that will be used for the optimization algorithm to adjust the different weights for the different perceptrons that will be part of your network. Hence, this is the function that will produce the quantity, and the goal of the optimizer is to make this quantity as small as possible.

- **Weight initialization strategy**: The weights for each perceptron in your network must be initialized with some values, and these values will be progressively changed by the optimization algorithm to minimize the loss. There are many ways in which you can initialize these values. You can initialize with all zeros. For many years, researchers used to initialize using a random normal distribution but, in recent years, researchers have come up with better choices, including Xavier initialization and He initialization.

- **Regularization strategy**: This is an optional but highly recommended function because deep learning models tend to overfit data due to the quantity of parameters that they calculate. You can use many choices, including the L1 regularization, L2 regularization, and dropout regularization strategies. In this book, we are not going to use regularization in our examples, but keep in mind that, if you want to build really effective deep learning models, you will very likely need a regularization strategy.

- **Training strategy**: The training strategy refers to the way the data will be presented to the training algorithm. This is not part of the model itself, but it will have an influence on the results and the performance of the model. When talking about training deep learning models, you will hear the word epoch. One epoch is one pass of all training examples through the network. In these deep learning models, you will have to present the data to the network many times so the network can learn the best parameters for the model. There is another concept here: batch size. This is the number of elements presented simultaneously to the training algorithm. So in the case of deep learning models, we don't present the whole training dataset to the model. What we do is we present batches of the dataset and, in each batch, we send just a few examples, maybe 100 or 50, and this is the way we train deep learning models. Now, you can use epoch and batch size to calculate the number of iterations that you will have in your model, and this is the number of training steps, which is the number of adjustments that the optimization algorithm makes to the weight in your model. So, for example, if you have 1,000 training examples and the batch size that you will use is 100, it will take 10 iterations to complete one epoch. You can get the total number of iterations with the following formula:

$$iterations = epochs \left\lceil \frac{T_{size}}{b} \right\rceil$$

So, there are a lot of decisions that you have to make as a modeler. These are very complex models and they can be very tricky to train. So, here is some guidance to consider before you start using these models:

- Because of the number of choices that we have in these models, they can be very tricky to build. So, they shouldn't be your first choice when trying to do predictions. Always begin with simpler and more understandable models, and then, if those models don't work, move to more complex models.
- There are best practices for all of the choices that we have seen, but you need more knowledge about these elements if you want to build effective deep learning models.
- For these models to perform really well, you need a lot of data. So, you cannot use these models with very small datasets.
- Learn more about the theory of these models to understand how to use them better. So if you really want to use these models for solving real-world problems, learning more about the theory behind these models is a must.

Introduction to TensorFlow

TensorFlow is an open source software library for numerical computation using data flow graphs. The concept of a computational graph is very important in TensorFlow and was specially designed for creating deep learning models. This library allows developers to deploy computations to one or more CPUs or GPUs in a desktop, a server, or even in mobile devices. This library was originally developed by researchers and engineers working at Google. It was open sourced in 2015 and, since then, it has become one of the major libraries in the machine learning world.

TensorFlow provides multiple APIs, and they can be categorized into the following two broad types:

- **Low level**: Also known as TensorFlow Core, this is the lowest-level API. This API gives us complete programming control and is aimed at researchers and users who need a high degree of flexibility when building their deep learning models.
- **High level**: High-level APIs such as `tf.contrib.learn`, `keras`, and TF-Slim are typically easier to use. They take care of repetitive tasks and low-level details that, as a high-level user, you don't need to worry about. They are designed for the fast implementation of commonly used models.

TensorFlow installation

Now, in preparation for our installation, we will create a new virtual environment in Anaconda. We can do so by using the following instructions:

1. We open the Anaconda prompt.
2. We type the following command line for creating a new virtual environment and pass the name of the environment with `anaconda`, which will install all of the packages that come with Anaconda:

```
conda create-n apa anaconda
```

Here `apa` stands for advanced predictive analytics. Installation can take some time depending on your internet speed.

3. Once the installation has been completed, type `activate apa` to activate the new virtual environment. Here is a screenshot of the Anaconda prompt, showing the installation of Anaconda packages:

```
conda create -n apa anaconda                                                      □   ×

(C:\Users\direc\Anaconda3) C:\Users\direc>conda create -n apa anaconda
Fetching package metadata ...........
Solving package specifications:
    zlib:              1.2.8-vc14_3        [vc14]

Proceed ([y]/n)? Y

INFO menuinst_win32:__init__(182): Menu: name: 'Anaconda${PY_VER} ${PLATFORM}', prefix: 'C:\Users\direc\Anaconda3\envs\a
pa', env_name: 'apa', mode: 'None', used_mode: 'user'
INFO menuinst_win32:__init__(182): Menu: name: 'Anaconda${PY_VER} ${PLATFORM}', prefix: 'C:\Users\direc\Anaconda3\envs\a
pa', env_name: 'apa', mode: 'None', used_mode: 'user'
INFO menuinst_win32:__init__(182): Menu: name: 'Anaconda${PY_VER} ${PLATFORM}', prefix: 'C:\Users\direc\Anaconda3\envs\a
pa', env_name: 'apa', mode: 'None', used_mode: 'user'
INFO menuinst_win32:__init__(182): Menu: name: 'Anaconda${PY_VER} ${PLATFORM}', prefix: 'C:\Users\direc\Anaconda3\envs\a
pa', env_name: 'apa', mode: 'None', used_mode: 'user'
INFO menuinst_win32:__init__(182): Menu: name: 'Anaconda${PY_VER} ${PLATFORM}', prefix: 'C:\Users\direc\Anaconda3\envs\a
pa', env_name: 'apa', mode: 'None', used_mode: 'user'
INFO menuinst_win32:__init__(182): Menu: name: 'Anaconda${PY_VER} ${PLATFORM}', prefix: 'C:\Users\direc\Anaconda3\envs\a
pa', env_name: 'apa', mode: 'None', used_mode: 'user'
INFO menuinst_win32:__init__(182): Menu: name: 'Anaconda${PY_VER} ${PLATFORM}', prefix: 'C:\Users\direc\Anaconda3\envs\a
pa', env_name: 'apa', mode: 'None', used_mode: 'user'
#
# To activate this environment, use:
# > activate apa
#
# To deactivate an active environment, use:
# > deactivate
#
# * for power-users using bash, you must source
#

(C:\Users\direc\Anaconda3) C:\Users\direc>activate apa

(apa) C:\Users\direc>
```

Now, the new virtual environment has been activated and we are ready to install TensorFlow inside this new virtual environment.

But before installing TensorFlow, you must know that there are basically following two installations of TensorFlow:

- TensorFlow with CPU support only
- TensorFlow with GPU support

The second option is usually faster because it uses the GPUs in your computer or your devices, but this installation needs **Nvidia** support. You also need additional software in order to run this installation and it is a little bit more complicated to install.

Here, for easiness, we will install and use the CPU version as there is no difference in writing a program and running it in the CPU or the GPU versions, apart from the speed. We use the following line of code to install TensorFlow in our system:

```
pip install --ignore-installed --upgrade tensorflow
```

On running the code, the installation of TensorFlow will be initiated and, once the installation is completed, you will see the following output on your screen:

```
Anaconda Prompt                                                                    —  □  ×
 Using cached tensorflow-1.3.0-cp36-cp36m-win_amd64.whl
Collecting protobuf>=3.3.0 (from tensorflow)
 Using cached protobuf-3.4.0-py2.py3-none-any.whl
Collecting six>=1.10.0 (from tensorflow)
 Using cached six-1.11.0-py2.py3-none-any.whl
Collecting numpy>=1.11.0 (from tensorflow)
 Using cached numpy-1.13.3-cp36-none-win_amd64.whl
Collecting wheel>=0.26 (from tensorflow)
 Using cached wheel-0.30.0-py2.py3-none-any.whl
Collecting tensorflow-tensorboard<0.2.0,>=0.1.0 (from tensorflow)
 Using cached tensorflow_tensorboard-0.1.8-py3-none-any.whl
Collecting setuptools (from protobuf>=3.3.0->tensorflow)
 Downloading setuptools-36.6.0-py2.py3-none-any.whl (481kB)
   100% |████████████████████████████████| 481kB 1.5MB/s
Collecting werkzeug>=0.11.10 (from tensorflow-tensorboard<0.2.0,>=0.1.0->tensorflow)
 Using cached Werkzeug-0.12.2-py2.py3-none-any.whl
Collecting markdown>=2.6.8 (from tensorflow-tensorboard<0.2.0,>=0.1.0->tensorflow)
Collecting bleach==1.5.0 (from tensorflow-tensorboard<0.2.0,>=0.1.0->tensorflow)
 Using cached bleach-1.5.0-py2.py3-none-any.whl
Collecting html5lib==0.9999999 (from tensorflow-tensorboard<0.2.0,>=0.1.0->tensorflow)
Installing collected packages: six, setuptools, protobuf, numpy, wheel, werkzeug, markdown, html5lib, bleach, tensorflow
-tensorboard, tensorflow
Successfully installed bleach-1.5.0 html5lib-0.9999999 markdown-2.6.9 numpy-1.13.3 protobuf-3.4.0 setuptools-36.6.0 six-
1.11.0 tensorflow-1.3.0 tensorflow-tensorboard-0.1.8 werkzeug-0.12.2 wheel-0.30.0

(apa) C:\Users\direc>
```

Now, we will start a Python shell to test the installation by performing the following steps:

1. We type `python` to start the Python shell.
2. We use `import tensorflow as tf` to import TensorFlow into our Python shell.
3. We run `hello = tf.constant("Hello")`; this will create a constant named `hello`.

4. We create a session using `sess = tf.Session()`.

 If you see similar warning messages to the ones in the following screenshot, you can ignore them, as they are just telling you that you could install with different options so TensorFlow may run faster.

5. Let's print the result of `hello` by running the constant within the session using `print(sess.run(hello))`:

```
(apa) C:\Users\direc>python
Python 3.6.1 |Anaconda 4.4.0 (64-bit)| (default, May 11 2017, 13:25:24) [MSC v.1900 64 bit (AMD64)] on win32
Type "help", "copyright", "credits" or "license" for more information.
>>> import tensorflow as tf
>>> hello = tf.Constant("Hello")
Traceback (most recent call last):
  File "<stdin>", line 1, in <module>
AttributeError: module 'tensorflow' has no attribute 'Constant'
>>> hello = tf.constant("Hello")
>>> sess = tf.Session()
2017-10-15 14:23:18.420603: W C:\tf_jenkins\home\workspace\rel-win\M\windows\PY\36\tensorflow\core\platform\cpu_feature_
guard.cc:45] The TensorFlow library wasn't compiled to use AVX instructions, but these are available on your machine and
 could speed up CPU computations.
2017-10-15 14:23:18.420872: W C:\tf_jenkins\home\workspace\rel-win\M\windows\PY\36\tensorflow\core\platform\cpu_feature_
guard.cc:45] The TensorFlow library wasn't compiled to use AVX2 instructions, but these are available on your machine an
d could speed up CPU computations.
>>> print(sess.run(hello))
b'Hello'
>>> _
```

If you get a result of `Hello`, similar to this screenshot, it means that our installation is correct. So, now we are ready to use TensorFlow to build some models.

Core concepts in TensorFlow

There are some major concepts that we need to understand before actually using the `tensorflow` library. The following are the concepts that we will cover in this book:

- Tensors
- Computational graphs
- Sessions
- Variables
- Placeholders
- Constants

Tensors

A **tensor** is the central unit of data in TensorFlow. A tensor consists of a set of primitive values shaped into an array of any number of dimensions. It is basically a multidimensional array similar to a NumPy array. The number of dimensions defines the rank of a tensor. Let's see some of the following examples:

- 3: If we have a single number, the tensor will be considered a rank 0 tensor. This can be a scalar with `shape[]`.
- `[2., 2., 1.]`: If we have a vector, it will be considered a rank 1 tensor, so this is what we call a vector of shape 3 because it has three elements.
- `[[9., 5., 3.], [4., 5., 7]]`: A matrix with shape `[2, 3]` would be a rank 2 tensor.
- `[[[8., 3.]], [[7., 9.,]]]`: A matrix with shape `[2, 1, 2]` would be a rank 3 tensor, as you can see in the outermost level we have two elements, then in the next level we have only one element, and in the last dimension, we have two elements. That's why we have 2, 1, and 2 as the values and these are all tensors.

Computational graph

A computational graph is a series of TensorFlow operations, also known as **ops**, arranged into a graph of nodes. The following two principle steps are used by TensorFlow Core:

1. Define a computational graph
2. Run the computational graph

Let's try to understand this concept with a very simple example. Let's say that you have a function with two variables, **x** and **y** as shown in the following screenshot:

$$f(x, y) = x^2 y + 4y$$

We will use the preceding formula to calculate or to build a computational graph for the actual value of this function when you pass the values **3** and 2 for **x** and **y** respectively:

$$f(3,2) = 3^2 \times 2 + 4 \times 2 = 26$$

Now, let's build a computational graph for actually getting the result from this computation model:

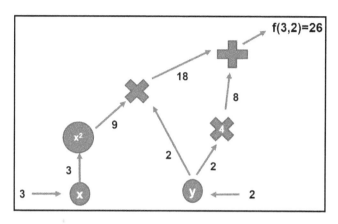

In the preceding screenshot, we see the values that flow through the computational graph to different nodes in the graph. So, in the first node, the value **3** gets assigned to **x** and, in the other node, the value **2** gets assigned to **y**. Now, the value of **x** flows to an operation node where it gets squared, and the result of that node flows to another operation where it gets multiplied to the value of **y**. We also have another node, where the value of **y** gets multiplied by **4**. The result of the **x** and **y** multiplication node and the result of the **y** multiplication node flow to the final node, which is the addition node, which gives us the final output **26**. So this is essentially how TensorFlow works. What flows between nodes are tensors.

There are other following objects that we use in TensorFlow:

- **Session**: A session is an object that encapsulates the environment in which operation objects are executed. So, sessions are objects that place operations onto devices such as CPUs or GPUs.
- **Placeholders**: A placeholder is a promise to provide a value later. These objects are usually used to provide training and testing values in machine learning models.
- **Variables**: These are objects that are initialized with a value, and that value can change during the execution of the graph. Typically, they are used as trainable variables in machine learning models.
- **Constants**: Constants are objects whose values never change.

To have a better understanding of these object concepts, let's see an example. First, we will import the required libraries by executing the following code snippet:

```
import tensorflow as tf
import numpy as np
import matplotlib.pyplot as plt
%matplotlib inline
```

We then define some TensorFlow objects, placeholders, and a constant by executing the following code snippet:

```
#Placeholders
x = tf.placeholder(tf.float32)
y = tf.placeholder(tf.float32)
c = tf.constant(5)
```

Here, we define a placeholder called x and another placeholder called y. You have to explicitly give the type of object that you will use in TensorFlow, which we have in our example as float32. We then define a constant, c ,whose value is 5.

After you create these objects, if you try to print them, you will not see the value of the object, but it will show the type of the object as shown in the following screenshot:

```
In [9]:  x

Out[9]:  <tf.Tensor 'Placeholder_2:0' shape=<unknown> dtype=float32>

In [10]:  c

Out[10]:  <tf.Tensor 'Const_1:0' shape=() dtype=int32>
```

Now, let's implement the following function with our placeholders:

$$f(x,y) = x^2 y + 4y$$

We will use the placeholders that we just created to define the different nodes for our graph by executing the following code lines:

```
square_node = x*x
mult_node = square_node*y
quadruple_node = 4*y
adder_node = mult_node + quadruple_node
```

Again, if you try to print the values of these objects, you will get the object type and not the values as shown in the following screenshot:

```
In [13]:  square_node    I

Out[13]:  <tf.Tensor 'mul_2:0' shape=<unknown> dtype=float32>
```

So, to perform the calculations for these objects, you must create a session object and then run all of the objects inside a session:

```
In [14]:  sess = tf.Session()

In [15]:  sess.run(c)

Out[15]:  5

In [16]:  sess.run(x, feed_dict={x:6})

Out[16]:  array(6.0, dtype=float32)

In [17]:  sess.run square_node, feed_dict={x:10}

Out[17]:  100.0

In [19]:  sess.run(adder_node, feed_dict={x:3, y:2})

Out[19]:  26.0
```

If you are doing some computations, you don't need to define the computational graph, as TensorFlow will do this behind the scenes. So, let's say that you want to calculate f and we print the value, it will still give the object type. But to actually see the value of f when you perform the computation, we will run the function in a session object again:

```
In [20]:  f = x**2 * y + 4*y

In [21]:  f

Out[21]:  <tf.Tensor 'add_1:0' shape=<unknown> dtype=float32>

In [22]:  sess.run f, feed_dict={x:3, y:2}

Out[22]:  26.0
```

There are two ways in which you can run objects in TensorFlow. There are other ways, but these are the basic and most common ways you can run objects. You can use the `run()` method from a session or you can use the `eval()` method from the tensor:

```
In [23]:  with tf.Session() as sess:
              print("f(10,5)=", sess.run(f, feed_dict={x:10, y:5}))
              print("f(10,5)=", f.eval(feed_dict={x:10, y:5}))

          f(10,5)= 520.0
          f(10,5)= 520.0
```

As we can see, we created a session using the `with` statement and ran those two methods inside this statement.

Now, we will build a basic linear model. We will have TensorFlow guess the best values for the `b` and `w` parameters shown in the following screenshot:

$$y = b + wx + noise$$

In the previous equation, the value of `w` is 5 and `b` is 1. We will use these values for training and plot the values on a scatter plot:

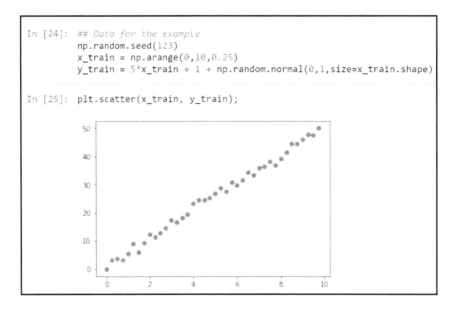

```
In [24]:  ## Data for the example
          np.random.seed(123)
          x_train = np.arange(0,10,0.25)
          y_train = 5*x_train + 1 + np.random.normal(0,1,size=x_train.shape)

In [25]:  plt.scatter(x_train, y_train);
```

As you can see, we have the linear relationship between the two values.

We will now initiate the variable objects, w and b ,with the value 0, and they will be our trainable parameters. The placeholders are usually the objects that we use to pass the data, so we will create two placeholders, x and y, and now the linear model will be one of the nodes in our computational graph. Then, we will define a `loss` function, which will be used by the optimizer to actually change the values of our variable. Every time we run the training operation, the optimizer will adjust the values of w and b in order to minimize the loss. We will then initialize the variables and create a session to run the `init` initializer node as shown in the following screenshot:

```
In [18]:  w = tf.Variable(0.0, dtype=tf.float32)
          b = tf.Variable(0.0, dtype=tf.float32)

In [19]:  x = tf.placeholder(tf.float32)
          y = tf.placeholder(tf.float32)

In [20]:  linear_model = w * x + b

In [21]:  loss = tf.reduce_sum(tf.square(linear_model - y))

In [22]:  optimizer = tf.train.GradientDescentOptimizer(learning_rate=0.0005)

In [23]:  training_op = optimizer.minimize(loss)

In [24]:  init = tf.global_variables_initializer()

In [25]:  sess = tf.Session()

In [26]:  sess.run(init)
```

Now, we can start training our machine learning model. We will run the training operation 20 times, which will make corrections to our values of w and b to minimize the loss:

```
In [35]:  for i in range(20):
              sess.run(training_op, feed_dict={x: x_train, y: y_train})
              print "Iteration {}: w: {:0.5f}, b: {:0.5f}".format(i, sess.run(w), sess.run(b))

          Iteration 0: w: 6.58667, b: 1.01166
          Iteration 1: w: 4.52043, b: 0.69846
          Iteration 2: w: 5.16780, b: 0.80070
          Iteration 3: w: 4.96417, b: 0.77262
          Iteration 4: w: 5.02743, b: 0.78537
          Iteration 5: w: 5.00699, b: 0.78527
          Iteration 6: w: 5.01281, b: 0.78916
          Iteration 7: w: 5.01040, b: 0.79176
          Iteration 8: w: 5.01058, b: 0.79473
          Iteration 9: w: 5.00995, b: 0.79754
          Iteration 10: w: 5.00958, b: 0.80036
          Iteration 11: w: 5.00913, b: 0.80315
          Iteration 12: w: 5.00872, b: 0.80590
          Iteration 13: w: 5.00830, b: 0.80863
          Iteration 14: w: 5.00788, b: 0.81134
          Iteration 15: w: 5.00747, b: 0.81401
          Iteration 16: w: 5.00707, b: 0.81666
          Iteration 17: w: 5.00667, b: 0.81928
          Iteration 18: w: 5.00627, b: 0.82187
          Iteration 19: w: 5.00588, b: 0.82444
```

As we see, after the first iteration, the optimizer corrected the values of w and b, which is also carried out in every iteration.

We can also do this using some linear algebra, but remember that the goal of machine learning is to actually learn the parameters from the data, and in this case, we have run our first machine learning model using TensorFlow.

Summary

In this chapter, we talked about ANNs, deep learning, and the elements of a deep learning model. We then installed TensorFlow and learned about the core concepts that we use in TensorFlow.

In the next chapter, we will perform predictive analytics with TensorFlow and deep learning.

5
Predictive Analytics with TensorFlow and Deep Neural Networks

TensorFlow is an open source library developed by **Google Brain Team**. It is used in large-scale machine learning applications, such as neural networks, and for making numerical computations. Developers are able to create dataflow graphs using TensorFlow. These graphs show the movement of data. TensorFlow can be used to train and run deep neural networks for various applications such as image recognition, machine language translation, and natural language processing.

We already know that predictive analytics is about providing predictions about unknown events. We are going to use it here with TensorFlow.

In this chapter, we will cover the following topics:

- Predictions with TensorFlow
- Regression with **Deep Neural networks** (**DNNs**)
- Classification with DNNs

Predictions with TensorFlow

We will perform the `hello world` example of deep learning. This example is used to check and ensure that a model is working as intended. For this, we will use the MNIST dataset.

Introduction to the MNIST dataset

MNIST stands for **Mixed National Institute of Standards and Technology**, which has produced a handwritten digits dataset. This is one of the most researched datasets in machine learning, and is used to classify handwritten digits. This dataset is helpful for predictive analytics because of its sheer size, allowing deep learning to work its magic efficiently. This dataset contains 60,000 training images and 10,000 testing images, formatted as 28 x 28 pixel monochrome images. The following screenshot shows the images contained in this dataset:

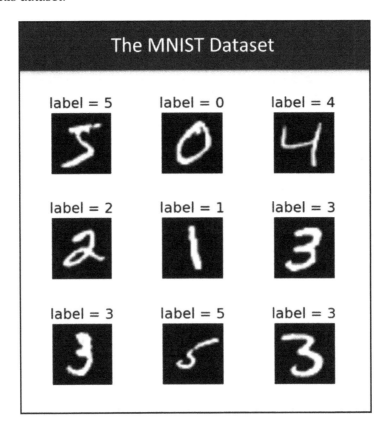

In the preceding screenshot, we can see that, for every handwritten digit, there is a corresponding true label; we can therefore use this dataset to build classification models. So we can use the image to classify each into one of the 10 digits from 0 to 9.

Building classification models using MNIST dataset

Let's take a look at the following steps and learn to build a classification model:

1. We have to import the libraries that we will use in this dataset. Use the following lines of code to import the `tensorflow`, `numpy`, and `matplotlib` libraries:

```
import tensorflow as tf
import numpy as np
import matplotlib.pyplot as plt

from tensorflow.contrib.layers import fully_connected

%matplotlib inline
```

2. We will import the `fully_connected` function, which we will be used to build the layers of our network, from `tensorflow.contrib.layers`.

Elements of the DNN model

Before running the model, we first have to determine the elements that we will use in building a multilayer perceptron model. Following are the elements that we will use in this model:

- **Architecture**: The model contains 728 neurons in the input layer. This is because we have 28 images and each image has 28 pixels. Here, each pixel is a feature in this case, so we have 728 pixels. We will have 10 elements in the output layer, and we will also use three hidden layers, although we could use any number of hidden layers. Here, we will use three hidden layers. The number of neurons we will use in each layer is 350 in the first layer, 200 in the second one, and 100 in the last layer.

- **Activation function**: We will use the ReLU activation function, as shown in the following code block:

```
vector = np.arange(-5,5,0.1)
def relu(x) :
return max(0.,x)
relu = np.vectorize(relu)
```

If the input is negative, the function outputs 0, and if the input is positive the function just outputs the same value as the input. So, mathematically, the ReLU function looks similar to this. The following screenshot shows the lines of code used for generating the graphical representation of the ReLU activation function:

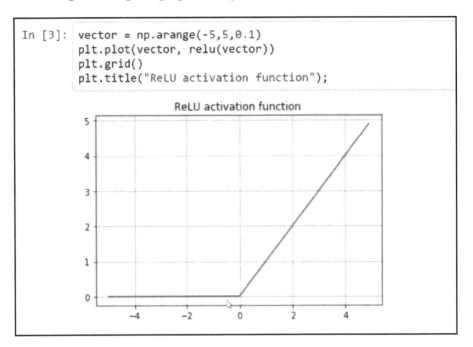

```
In [3]: vector = np.arange(-5,5,0.1)
        plt.plot(vector, relu(vector))
        plt.grid()
        plt.title("ReLU activation function");
```

It gains the maximum between 0 and the input. This activation function will be used in every neuron of the hidden layers.

- **Optimizing algorithm**: The optimizing algorithm used here is the gradient descent with a learning rate of 0.01.
- **Loss function**: For the `loss` function, we will use the `cross_entropy` function, but as with other loss functions that we have used in this book, this function measures the distance between the actual values and the predictions that the model makes.
- **Weights initialization strategy**: For this, we will use the Xavier initializer, a method that actually comes with the `fully_connected` function from TensorFlow as a default.
- **Regularization strategy**: We are not going to use any regularization strategy.

- **Training strategy**: We are going to use 20 epochs. The dataset will be presented to the network 20 times, and in every iteration, we will use a batch size of 80. So, we will present the data to the network 80 points at a time and the whole dataset 20 times.

Building the DNN

Now we will import the dataset that we are going to use. The reason for using this dataset is that it is easily available. We are going to actually use this dataset and build a DNN model around it. In the next sections, we will see the steps involved in building a DNN model.

Reading the data

Here, we read data in the cell. The following screenshot shows the lines of code used to read the data:

Reading the data

```
In [4]: from tensorflow.examples.tutorials.mnist import input_data
        mnist = input_data.read_data_sets("./data/")

        Extracting ./data/train-images-idx3-ubyte.gz
        Extracting ./data/train-labels-idx1-ubyte.gz
        Extracting ./data/t10k-images-idx3-ubyte.gz
        Extracting ./data/t10k-labels-idx1-ubyte.gz
```

Defining the architecture

We will use three hidden layers, with 256 neurons for the first layer, 128 for the second, and 64 for the third one. The following code snippet shows the architecture for the classification example:

```
n_inputs = 28*28
n_hidden1 = 350
n_hidden2 = 200
n_hidden3 = 100
n_outputs = 10
```

Placeholders for inputs and labels

The values of different layers are the objects, and are also called placeholders for inputs and labels. These placeholders are used for feeding the data into the network. The following lines of code are used for showing placeholders for the inputs and labels:

```
X = tf.placeholder(tf.float32, shape=[None, n_inputs])
y = tf.placeholder(tf.int64)
```

So we have a placeholder X for the features, which is the input layer, and we have a placeholder y for the target value. So this object will contain the actual true labels of the digits.

Building the neural network

For building DNNs, we use the `fully_connected` function for the first hidden layer. The input for this hidden layer is x, which is the data from the placeholder. `n_hidden1` is the number of neurons that we have in this hidden layer, which you will remember is 350 neurons. Now, this hidden layer 1 becomes the input for the hidden layer 2, and `n_hidden2` is the number of neurons in this layer. Likewise, hidden layer 2 becomes the input for the third hidden layer and we will use this number of neurons in this layer. Finally, the output layer, which we will call `logits`, is the fully connected layer that we use as input, hidden layer 3. The following screenshot shows the lines of code used for building the neural network:

Building the DNN

```
In [ ]: hidden1 = fully_connected(X, n_hidden1)
        hidden2 = fully_connected(hidden1, n_hidden2)
        hidden3 = fully_connected(hidden2, n_hidden3)
        logits = fully_connected(hidden3, n_outputs, activation_fn=None)
```

We enter the output as 10 because we have 10 categories in our classification problem and we know that in the output layer we don't use any activation function.

The loss function

For our `loss` function, we use the cross-entropy function. TensorFlow provides us with many such functions. For example, in this case, we are using the `sparse_softmax_cross_entropy _with_logits` function because here we got `logits` from the network. So, in this function, we pass the actual labels. These are the true labels, which are `logits`—the results or the output of our network. The following screenshot shows the lines of code used for showing the use of the `reduce_mean` function with this cross-entropy for getting the loss:

Loss function

```
In [ ]:  cross_entropy = tf.nn.sparse_softmax_cross_entropy_with_logits(
                            labels=y, logits=logits)
         loss = tf.reduce_mean(cross_entropy)
```

Now, using this cross-entropy, we can calculate the loss as the mean of the vector that we will get here. So this is the `loss` function and the mean of the cross-entropy.

Defining optimizer and training operations

The goal of the optimizer is to minimize the loss, and it does this by adjusting the different weights that we have in all the layers of our network. The optimizer used here is the gradient descent with a learning rate of 0.01. The following screenshot shows the lines of code used for defining the optimizer and also shows the training operations.

Optimizer & training operation

```
In [9]:  learning_rate = 0.01
         optimizer = tf.train.GradientDescentOptimizer(learning_rate)
         training_op = optimizer.minimize(loss)
```

Each time we run the training operation `training_op`, the optimizer will change the values of these weights a little bit. In doing so, it minimizes the loss, and the predictions and the actual values are as close as possible.

Training strategy and valuation of accuracy of the classification

Here we set the training strategy. We will use 20 epochs with a batch size of 80. In all of these cells, we have build the computational graph that will be used in this program. The following screenshot shows the lines of code used for showing the training strategy and the couple of nodes for evaluating the accuracy of the classification:

Evaluation of the accuracy of the classification

```
In [ ]:  correct = tf.nn.in_top_k(predictions=logits, targets=y, k=1)
         accuracy = tf.reduce_mean(tf.cast(correct, tf.float32))
```

Training strategy

```
In [ ]:  n_epochs = 20
         batch_size = 80
```

Running the computational graph

For actually running the computational graph, first we will initialize all the variables in our program. The following screenshot shows the lines of code used for running the computational graph:

Running the computational graph

```
In [ ]:    1  with tf.Session() as sess:
           2      ## Initializing the variables
           3      tf.global_variables_initializer().run()
           4      for epoch in range(n_epochs):
           5          for iteration in range(mnist.train.num_examples // batch_size):
           6              X_batch, y_batch = mnist.train.next_batch(batch_size)
           7              sess.run(training_op, feed_dict={X: X_batch, y: y_batch})
           8          acc_train = accuracy.eval(feed_dict={X: X_batch, y: y_batch})
           9          acc_test = accuracy.eval(feed_dict={X: mnist.test.images, y: mnist.test.labels})
          10          print("======= Epoch: {} ========".format(epoch+1))
          11          print("Train accuracy:", acc_train, "| Test accuracy:", acc_test)
          12          print(50*"-")
          13      print("Done Trainning!")
          14
          15      ## Producing individual predictions
          16      print("\n=====================\n")
          17      print("Using the network to make individual predictions")
          18      n_pred = 15
          19      X_new = mnist.test.images[:n_pred]
          20      Z = logits.eval(feed_dict={X: X_new})
          21      y_pred = np.argmax(Z, axis=1)
          22      print("Actual | Predicted")
          23      print("=====================")
          24      for obs, pred in zip(mnist.test.labels[:n_pred], y_pred):
```

In line 3, we initialize all the variables in our program. Now, here, we don't have any variables explicitly. However, the variables that are inside are fully connected. The `fully_connected` function is where we have all the hidden layers that contain the weights. These are the variables which is why we must initialize the variables with the `global_ variables_initializer` object and run this node. For each epoch, we run this loop 20 times. Now, for each iteration that we have in the number of examples over the batch size, which is 80, we get the values for the features and the targets. So this will be 80 data points for each iteration. Then, we run the training operation and will pass as x; we will pass the feature values and here we will pass the target values. Remember, x and y are our placeholders. Then, we evaluate the accuracy of the training and then evaluate the accuracy in the testing dataset, and we get the testing dataset. We get from `mnist.test.images`, and so these are now the features and `test.labels` are the targets. Then, we print the two accuracies after these two loops are completed.

We then produce some individual predictions for the first 15 images in the testing dataset. After running this, we get the first epoch, with a training accuracy of 86 percent and a testing accuracy of 88-89 percent. The following screenshot shows the results of training and the testing results for different epochs:

```
======= Epoch: 1 ========                              ======= Epoch: 11 ========
Train accuracy: 0.8625 | Test accuracy: 0.8898         Train accuracy: 0.975 | Test accuracy: 0.9602
--------------------------------------------           ------------------------------------------------
======= Epoch: 2 ========                              ======= Epoch: 12 ========
Train accuracy: 0.9875 | Test accuracy: 0.9151         Train accuracy: 0.975 | Test accuracy: 0.9594
--------------------------------------------           ------------------------------------------------
======= Epoch: 3 ========                              ======= Epoch: 13 ========
Train accuracy: 0.925 | Test accuracy: 0.9249          Train accuracy: 0.95 | Test accuracy: 0.961
--------------------------------------------           ------------------------------------------------
======= Epoch: 4 ========                              ======= Epoch: 14 ========
Train accuracy: 0.95 | Test accuracy: 0.9351           Train accuracy: 1.0 | Test accuracy: 0.9642
--------------------------------------------           ------------------------------------------------
======= Epoch: 5 ========                              ======= Epoch: 15 ========
Train accuracy: 0.9125 | Test accuracy: 0.9405         Train accuracy: 0.9875 | Test accuracy: 0.9654
--------------------------------------------           ------------------------------------------------
======= Epoch: 6 ========                              ======= Epoch: 16 ========
Train accuracy: 0.95 | Test accuracy: 0.9425           Train accuracy: 0.95 | Test accuracy: 0.9661
--------------------------------------------           ------------------------------------------------
======= Epoch: 7 ========                              ======= Epoch: 17 ========
Train accuracy: 0.9875 | Test accuracy: 0.9499         Train accuracy: 0.975 | Test accuracy: 0.9662
--------------------------------------------           ------------------------------------------------
======= Epoch: 8 ========                              ======= Epoch: 18 ========
Train accuracy: 0.9875 | Test accuracy: 0.9525         Train accuracy: 0.975 | Test accuracy: 0.9684
--------------------------------------------           ------------------------------------------------
======= Epoch: 9 ========                              ======= Epoch: 19 ========
Train accuracy: 0.975 | Test accuracy: 0.9556          Train accuracy: 0.9625 | Test accuracy: 0.9691
--------------------------------------------           ------------------------------------------------
======= Epoch: 10 ========                             ======= Epoch: 20 ========
Train accuracy: 0.9375 | Test accuracy: 0.9566         Train accuracy: 0.975 | Test accuracy: 0.9695
--------------------------------------------           ------------------------------------------------
```

The programs takes a little bit of time to run, but after 20 epochs, the testing accuracy is almost 97 percent. The following screenshot shows the actual labels and the predicted labels. These are the predictions the network made:

```
Using the network to make individual predictions
Actual | Predicted
======================
    7  | 1   7
    2  |     2
    1  |     1
    0  |     0
    4  |     4
    1  |     1
    4  |     4
    9  |     9
    5  |     6
    9  |     9
    0  |     0
    6  |     6
    9  |     9
    0  |     0
    1  |     1
```

So we have built our first DNN model and we were able to classify handwritten digits using this program with almost 97 percent accuracy.

Regression with Deep Neural Networks (DNN)

For regression with DNNs, we first have to import the libraries we will use here. We will import TensorFlow, pandas, NumPy, and matplotlib with the lines of code shown in the following screenshot:

```
In [1]:  import tensorflow as tf
         import pandas as pd
         import numpy as np
         import matplotlib.pyplot as plt

         from sklearn.model_selection import train_test_split
         from tensorflow.contrib.layers import fully_connected

         %matplotlib inline
```

We will use the `fully_ connected` function from the `tensorflow.contrib.layers` model.

Elements of the DNN model

Before running the model, we first have to determine the elements that we will use in building a multilayer perceptron model, shown as follows:

- **Architecture:** The model contains 23 elements in the input layer, hence we have 25 features in this dataset. We have only one element in the output layer and we will use three hidden layers, although we could use any number of hidden layers. We will use 256 neurons for the first layer, 128 for the second, and 64 for the third one. These are the powers of two.
- **Activation function:** We will choose the ReLu activation function.
- **Optimizing algorithm**: The optimization algorithm used here is the Adam optimizer. The Adam optimizer is one of the most popular optimizers as it is the best option for a lot of problems.
- **Loss function**: We will use the mean squared error because we are doing a regression problem here and this is one of the optimal choices for the `loss` function.
- **Weights initialization strategy:** For this, we will use the Xavier initializer, which comes as the default that with the `fully_connected` function from TensorFlow.
- **Regularization strategy**: We are not going to use any regularization strategy.
- **Training strategy**: We are going to use 40 epochs. We will present the dataset 40 times to the network and, in every iteration, we will use batches of 50 data points each time we run the training operation. So, we will use 50 elements of the dataset.

Building the DNN

First, we import the dataset that we will use. The reason behind using this dataset is that, it is easily available. The following are the steps involved in building a DNN model.

Reading the data

We are going to read data in the cell and filter it to our preference. The following screenshot shows the lines of code used to read the data:

```
In [2]:  data_path= '../data/diamonds.csv'
         diamonds = pd.read_csv(data_path)
         diamonds = pd.concat([diamonds, pd.get_dummies(diamonds['cut'], prefix='cut', drop_first=True)],axis=1)
         diamonds = pd.concat([diamonds, pd.get_dummies(diamonds['color'], prefix='color', drop_first=True)],axi
         diamonds = pd.concat([diamonds, pd.get_dummies(diamonds['clarity'], prefix='clarity', drop_first=True)]
         diamonds.drop(['cut','color','clarity'], axis=1, inplace=True)
```

Objects for modeling

After importing the datasets, we prepare the objects for modeling. So we have training and testing here for x and for y. The following screenshot shows the lines of code used to prepare the objects for modelling:

```
In [3]:  from sklearn.preprocessing import RobustScaler
         target_name = 'price'
         robust_scaler = RobustScaler()
         X = diamonds.drop('price', axis=1)
         X = robust_scaler.fit_transform(X)
         y = diamonds[target_name]
         X_train, X_test, y_train, y_test = train_test_split(X, y, test_size=0.1, random_state=123)
```

Training strategy

This is the training strategy with 40 epochs and a batch size of 50. This is created with the following lines of code:

```
n_epochs = 40
batch_size = 50
```

Input pipeline for the DNN

Since this is an external dataset, we have to use a data input pipeline, and TensorFlow provides different tools for getting data inside the deep learning model. Here, we create a dataset object and an iterator object with the lines of code shown in the following screenshot:

```
In [5]: X_placeholder = tf.placeholder(X_train.dtype, shape=X_train.shape)
        y_placeholder = tf.placeholder(y_train.dtype, shape=y_train.shape)

        dataset = tf.contrib.data.Dataset.from_tensor_slices((X_placeholder, y_placeholder))
        dataset = dataset.shuffle(buffer_size=10000)
        dataset = dataset.batch(batch_size)
        iterator = dataset.make_initializable_iterator()
        next_element = iterator.get_next()
```

First, we produce the dataset object. Then, we pass the whole training dataset to some placeholders that we will use. Then, we shuffle the data and divide or partition the training dataset into batches of 50. Hence, the dataset object is prepared, containing all of the training samples partitioned into batches of size 50. Next, we make an iterator object. Then, with the `get_next` method, we create a node called `next_element`, which provides the batches of 50 from the training examples.

Defining the architecture

We use three hidden layers with 256 neurons for the first layer, 128 for the second, and 64 for the third one. The following code snippet shows the architecture for this procedure:

```
n_inputs = X_train.shape[1] #23
n_hidden1 = 256
n_hidden2 = 128
n_hidden3 = 64
n_outputs = 1
```

Placeholders for input values and labels

The values of different layers are the objects, also called the placeholders, for inputs and labels. These placeholders are used for feeding the data into the network. The following lines of code shows the placeholders for inputs and labels:

```
X = tf.placeholder(X_train.dtype, shape=[None,n_inputs])
y = tf.placeholder(y_train.dtype)
```

Building the DNN

For building the following example, we first have to define the DNN function. This function will take X_values and output the predictions. For the first hidden layer, we use a `fully_connected` function. The input for this hidden layer will be X, which is the data that comes from the placeholder, and `n_hidden1` is the number of neurons that we have in this hidden layer. Remember we have 350 neurons in the first hidden layer. Now, the first hidden layer becomes the input for the second hidden layer, and `n_hidden2` is the number of neurons that we use in this second hidden layer. Likewise, this second hidden layer becomes the input for the third hidden layer and we use this number of neurons in this layer. Finally, we have the output layer, let's call it `y_pred`, and this is a fully connected layer, with the third hidden layer as input. This is one output and this layer has no activation function. The following screenshot shows the lines of code used for building the neural network:

Building the DNN

```
In [8]:  def DNN(X_values):
             hidden1 = fully_connected(X_values, n_hidden1)
             hidden2 = fully_connected(hidden1, n_hidden2)
             hidden3 = fully_connected(hidden2, n_hidden3)
             y_pred = fully_connected(hidden3, n_outputs, activation_fn=None)
             return tf.squeeze(y_pred)
```

The loss function

We will use the `mean_squared _error` function—TensorFlow provides us with many such functions. We pass the observed values and the predicted values and this function calculates the mean squared error. The following screenshot shows the lines of code used for showing the `mean_squared _error` function:

```
In [9]:  y_pred = DNN(X)
         loss = tf.losses.mean_squared_error(labels=y, predictions=y_pred)
```

Defining optimizer and training operations

The goal of the optimizer is to minimize the loss and it does this by adjusting the different weights that we have in all of the layers of our network. The optimizer used here is the Adam optimizer with a learning rate of 0.001.

The following screenshot shows the lines of code used for defining the optimizer and also shows the training operations:

```
In [10]:  optimizer = tf.train.AdamOptimizer()
          training_op = optimizer.minimize(loss)
```

The following screenshot shows some of the NumPy arrays that we created and will use for evaluation purposes:

```
In [11]:  train_mse = np.zeros(n_epochs)
          test_mse = np.zeros(n_epochs)
```

Running the computational graph

For actually running the computational graph, first we will initialize all of the variables in our program. The following screenshot shows the lines of code used for running the computational graph:

```
In [12]: with tf.Session() as sess:
             tf.global_variables_initializer().run()
             for epoch in range(n_epochs):
                 sess.run(iterator.initializer, feed_dict={X_placeholder: X_train, y_placeholder: y_train})
                 while True:
                     try:
                         batch_data = sess.run(next_element)
                         X_batch = batch_data[0]
                         y_batch = batch_data[1]
                         sess.run(training_op, feed_dict={X: X_batch, y:y_batch})
                     except tf.errors.OutOfRangeError:
                         break
                 print("=============EPOCH {}============".format(epoch+1))
                 train_mse[epoch] = loss.eval(feed_dict={X:X_batch, y:y_batch})
                 test_mse[epoch] = loss.eval(feed_dict={X:X_test, y:y_test})
                 print('Training MSE:', round(train_mse[epoch],1))
                 print('Test MSE:', round(test_mse[epoch],1))
             print("Done Trainning")

             ## Producing individual predictions
             print("\n======================\n")
             print("Using the network to make individual predictions")
             n_pred = 25
             y_obs = y_test[:n_pred]
             y_predicted = y_pred.eval(feed_dict={X:X_test[:n_pred,]})
             print("Actual | Predicted")
             print("======================")
             for obs, pred in zip(y_obs, y_predicted):
                 print("{: >8}   |{: >8}".format(round(obs), round(pred)))
             print("Correlation: ", np.corrcoef(y_obs, y_predicted)[0,1])
```

The variables are the weights that are implicit in the `fully_connected` function. Then, for every epoch, we initialize the iterator object and pass the training dataset. Here, we have `batch_data`, we run this `next_ element` node, and we get batches of 50. We can get the feature values and the labels, we can get the labels, and then we can run the training operation. When the object runs out of data, we get an error. In this case, when we get one of these errors, it means that we have used all of the training datasets. We then break from this `while` loop and proceed to the next epoch. Later, we produce some individual predictions so you can take a look at concrete predictions that this neural network makes.

The following screenshot shows the behavior of the training and the testing MSE of all 40 epochs as we present the data to this network:

```
=============EPOCH 1=============  =============EPOCH 15=============  =============EPOCH 29=============
Training MSE: 1108550.2            Training MSE: 592405.4             Training MSE: 133975.9
Test MSE: 931511.3                 Test MSE: 362381.4                 Test MSE: 319997.7
=============EPOCH 2=============  =============EPOCH 16=============  =============EPOCH 30=============
Training MSE: 881021.8             Training MSE: 255663.3             Training MSE: 341670.3
Test MSE: 778131.9                 Test MSE: 355960.6                 Test MSE: 319737.8
=============EPOCH 3=============  =============EPOCH 17=============  =============EPOCH 31=============
Training MSE: 702804.2             Training MSE: 417954.0             Training MSE: 202358.5
Test MSE: 704648.3                 Test MSE: 352198.5                 Test MSE: 313453.7
=============EPOCH 4=============  =============EPOCH 18=============  =============EPOCH 32=============
Training MSE: 611540.9             Training MSE: 337082.1             Training MSE: 888398.9
Test MSE: 648722.7                 Test MSE: 352286.7                 Test MSE: 363695.1
=============EPOCH 5=============  =============EPOCH 19=============  =============EPOCH 33=============
Training MSE: 256313.5             Training MSE: 95978.4              Training MSE: 331596.2
Test MSE: 622554.6                 Test MSE: 356439.2                 Test MSE: 326987.9
=============EPOCH 6=============  =============EPOCH 20=============  =============EPOCH 34=============
Training MSE: 100608.6             Training MSE: 285838.7             Training MSE: 190857.3
Test MSE: 585122.8                 Test MSE: 342621.8                 Test MSE: 322487.9
=============EPOCH 7=============  =============EPOCH 21=============  =============EPOCH 35=============
Training MSE: 773358.4             Training MSE: 442753.2             Training MSE: 214686.9
Test MSE: 554501.8                 Test MSE: 345900.2                 Test MSE: 328078.7
=============EPOCH 8=============  =============EPOCH 22=============  =============EPOCH 36=============
Training MSE: 191780.5             Training MSE: 251773.6             Training MSE: 151052.2
Test MSE: 522423.2                 Test MSE: 336092.2                 Test MSE: 328686.4
=============EPOCH 9=============  =============EPOCH 23=============  =============EPOCH 37=============
Training MSE: 856595.5             Training MSE: 277893.1             Training MSE: 243469.2
Test MSE: 563310.8                 Test MSE: 328649.6                 Test MSE: 319324.0
=============EPOCH 10=============  =============EPOCH 24=============  =============EPOCH 38=============
Training MSE: 309464.5             Training MSE: 246889.6             Training MSE: 81571.8
Test MSE: 477155.2                 Test MSE: 333666.9                 Test MSE: 314596.3
=============EPOCH 11=============  =============EPOCH 25=============  =============EPOCH 39=============
Training MSE: 543775.5             Training MSE: 339514.6             Training MSE: 278487.6
Test MSE: 449225.3                 Test MSE: 325606.8                 Test MSE: 315318.3
=============EPOCH 12=============  =============EPOCH 26=============  =============EPOCH 40=============
Training MSE: 193492.2             Training MSE: 88994.0              Training MSE: 294473.1
Test MSE: 431795.3                 Test MSE: 327290.8                 Test MSE: 329880.5
=============EPOCH 13=============  =============EPOCH 27=============  Done Trainning
Training MSE: 373994.0             Training MSE: 684625.6
Test MSE: 410921.5                 Test MSE: 369962.0                 =====================
=============EPOCH 14=============  =============EPOCH 28=============
Training MSE: 225274.2             Training MSE: 249729.0
                                   Test MSE: 322820.4
```

In the last tested MSE (epoch 40) we get the final value of the training and the testing MSE.

We get the actual predictions from the network and the values are relatively close. Here, we can see the predicted prices. For cheap diamonds, the network produced values that are relatively close. For very expensive diamonds, the network produced high values. Also, the predicted values are pretty close to the observed values. The following screenshot shows the actual and the predicted values that we got from the network:

```
Using the network to make individual predictions
Actual | Predicted
======================
    802 |     706.0
    935 |     865.0
   5826 |    6124.0
    935 |    1018.0
   2817 |    3144.0
    855 |     724.0
   2846 |    2808.0
    926 |     893.0
  15962 |   16339.0
   5445 |    5536.0
   2550 |    2271.0
   6221 |    5743.0
    544 |     570.0
   1122 |     804.0
   1367 |    1421.0
   4077 |    3992.0
   2144 |    1973.0
   2960 |    2735.0
   7131 |    7853.0
   1221 |    1239.0
   4563 |    5521.0
   3830 |    3764.0
   1137 |    1076.0
   1361 |    1386.0
   4641 |    4639.0
Correlation:  0.996551814653
```

The following screenshot shows the graph of the training MSE with the testing MSE and the lines of code used to produce it:

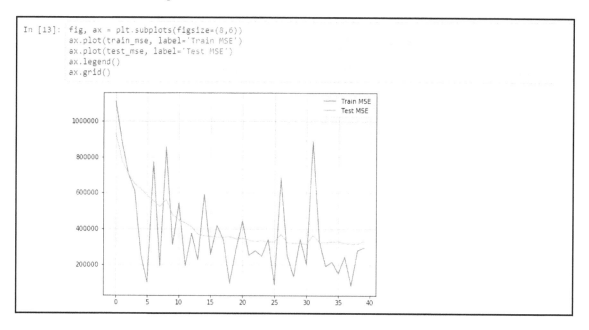

```
In [13]:  fig, ax = plt.subplots(figsize=(8,6))
          ax.plot(train_mse, label='Train MSE')
          ax.plot(test_mse, label='Test MSE')
          ax.legend()
          ax.grid()
```

Classification with DNNs

For understanding classification with DNNs, we first have to understand the concept of exponential linear unit function and the elements of the model.

Exponential linear unit activation function

The **Exponential Linear Unit** (**ELU**) function is a relatively recent modification to the ReLU function. It looks very similar to the ReLU function, but it has very different mathematical properties. The following screenshot shows the ELU function:

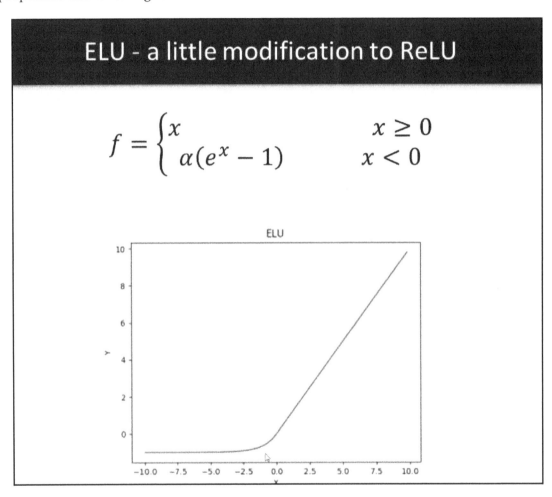

The preceding screenshot shows that, at 0, we don't have a corner. In the case of the ReLU function, we have a corner. In this function, instead of a single value going to 0, we have the ELU function slowly going to the negative alpha parameter.

Classification with DNNs

For classification with DNNs, we first have to import the libraries that we will use. Use the lines of code in the following screenshot to import the `tensorflow`, `pandas`, `numpy`, and `matplotlib` libraries:

```
In [1]:   import tensorflow as tf
          import pandas as pd
          import numpy as np
          import matplotlib.pyplot as plt

          from sklearn.model_selection import train_test_split
          from sklearn.preprocessing import RobustScaler
          from sklearn.metrics import precision_score, recall_score, accuracy_score

          from tensorflow.contrib.layers import fully_connected

          %matplotlib inline
```

We will also import the `train_test_split` function from `sklearn.model_selection`, `RobustScaler` from `sklearn.preprocessiong`, and `precision_score`, `recall_score`, and `accuracy_score` from `sklearn.metrics`. We also import the `fully_connected` function from `tensorflow.contrib.layers` to build the layers of our network.

Elements of the DNN model

Before running the model, we first have to determine the elements that we will use in building a multilayer perceptron model, shown as follows:

- **Architecture**: The model contains 25 elements in the input layer because we have 25 features in the dataset. We have two elements in the output layer and we will also use three hidden layers, although we could use any number of hidden layers. We will use the same number of neurons in each layer, 200. Here we use the powers of 2, which is an arbitrary choice.

- **Activation function**: We will choose the ELU activation function, which was explained in the preceding chapter.
- **Optimizing algorithm**: The optimization algorithm used here is the Adam optimizer with a learning rate of 0.001.
- **Loss function**: For the `loss` function, we will use the cross-entropy function.
- **Weights initialization strategy**: For this, we will use the Xavier initializer, a method that comes as default with the `fully_connected` function from TensorFlow.
- **Regularization strategy**: We are not going to use any regularization strategy.
- **Training strategy**: We are going to use 40 epochs. So, we will present the dataset 40 times to the network, and in every iteration, we will use a batch size of 100.

Building the DNN

Now, we import the dataset that we will use. The reason behind using this dataset is that it is easily available. The following are the steps involved in building a DNN model.

Reading the data

We are going to read the data in the cell. The following screenshot shows the lines of code used
to read the data:

```
In [2]:  default = pd.read_csv('../data/credit_card_default.csv', index_col="ID")
         default.rename(columns=lambda x: x.lower(), inplace=True)
         default.rename(columns={'pay_0':'pay_1','default payment next month':'default'}, inplace=True)
         # Base values: female, other_education, not_married
         default['grad_school'] = (default['education'] == 1).astype('int')
         default['university'] = (default['education'] == 2).astype('int')
         default['high_school'] = (default['education'] == 3).astype('int')
         default.drop('education', axis=1, inplace=True)

         default['male'] = (default['sex']==1).astype('int')
         default.drop('sex', axis=1, inplace=True)

         default['married'] = (default['marriage'] == 1).astype('int')
         default.drop('marriage', axis=1, inplace=True)

         # For pay_n features if >0 then it means the customer was delayed on that month
         pay_features = ['pay_' + str(i) for i in range(1,7)]
         for p in pay_features:
             default[p] = (default[p] > 0).astype(int)
```

Chapter 5

Producing the objects for modeling

Now, we produce the objects used for modeling. We are going to use 10 percent for testing and 90 percent for training. The following screenshot shows the lines of code used for producing the objects for modeling:

```
In [3]:  target_name = 'default'
         X = default.drop('default', axis=1)
         feature_names = X.columns
         robust_scaler = RobustScaler()
         X = robust_scaler.fit_transform(X)
         y = default[target_name]
         X_train, X_test, y_train, y_test = train_test_split(X, y, test_size=0.1, random_state=12, stratify=y)
```

Training strategy

This is the training strategy that we previously mentioned, 40 epochs and a batch size of 100. The following code block shows the parameters we set in this strategy:

```
n_epochs = 40
batch_size = 100
```

Input pipeline for DNN

Now, we perform the same thing that we did with the regression example. We create a `dataset` object and an iterator object. In the end, we have `next_element`. This will be a node in our computational graph that will give us 100 data points each time. Hence, we get the batches. The following screenshot shows the lines of code used for producing an input pipeline for the DNN:

```
In [5]:  X_placeholder = tf.placeholder(X_train.dtype, shape=X_train.shape)
         y_placeholder = tf.placeholder(y_train.dtype, shape=y_train.shape)

         dataset = tf.contrib.data.Dataset.from_tensor_slices((X_placeholder, y_placeholder))
         dataset = dataset.shuffle(buffer_size=10000)
         dataset = dataset.batch(batch_size)
         iterator = dataset.make_initializable_iterator()
         next_element = iterator.get_next()
```

Defining the architecture

We will use three hidden layers and 200 neurons for all three. The following code snippet shows the architecture we will use in this example:

```
n_inputs = X_train.shape[1]  #25
n_hidden1 = 200
n_hidden2 = 200
n_hidden3 = 200
n_outputs = 2
```

Placeholders for inputs and labels

The values of different layers are the objects, also called the placeholders, for inputs and labels. These placeholders are used for feeding the data into the network. The following lines of code are used for showing placeholders for inputs and labels:

```
X = tf.placeholder(X_train.dtype, shape=[None,n_inputs])
y = tf.placeholder(y_train.dtype)
```

Building the neural network

For building deep neural networks, we will use the DNN function. We have three layers and we will use the ELU function as the activation function. You can get this function from TensorFlow, `tf.nn.elu`, from which you can get a lot of functions that will help you build your deep learning models. The following screenshot shows the lines of code used for producing this function and for getting the output in the form of `logits`:

```
In [21]:  def DNN(X_values):
              hidden1 = fully_connected(X_values, n_hidden1, activation_fn=tf.nn.elu)
              hidden2 = fully_connected(hidden1, n_hidden2, activation_fn=tf.nn.elu)
              hidden3 = fully_connected(hidden2, n_hidden3, activation_fn=tf.nn.elu)
              logits = fully_connected(hidden3, n_outputs, activation_fn=None)
              return tf.cast(logits, dtype=tf.float32)
```

The final layer is called the `logits` layer. We won't be using any activation function in this layer.

The loss function

For the `loss` function, again, we are going to get `logits` from the DNN and then pass this `logits` to the `softmax_cross_entropy_with_logits`function from TensorFlow. We pass the true labels and `logits`, and then we can get the loss by using the `reduce_mean` function with `cross_entropy`. The following screenshot shows the lines of code used for showing the use of the `reduce_mean`function with `cross_entropy` for getting the loss:

```
In [22]:  logits = DNN(X)
          cross_entropy = tf.nn.sparse_softmax_cross_entropy_with_logits(labels=y, logits=logits
          loss = tf.reduce_mean(cross_entropy)
```

Evaluation nodes

Now, for evaluation, we will calculate the probabilities of default and non-default variables; you can get the probabilities by applying a `softmax` function to `logits`. The following screenshot shows the `softmax` function:

```
In [23]:  probs = tf.nn.softmax(logits)
```

$$softmax(x_i) = \frac{e^{x_i}}{\sum_{i=1}^{n} e^{x_i}}$$

The `softmax` function is used for providing the probabilities for the different categories.

Optimizer and the training operation

The goal of the optimizer is to minimize loss, and it does this by adjusting the different weights that we have in all of the layers of our network.

The following screenshot shows the lines of code used for defining the optimizer and shows the training operations:

```
In [24]:  optimizer = tf.train.AdamOptimizer(learning_rate=0.001)
          training_op = optimizer.minimize(loss)
```

In this case, the optimizer is, again, the Adam optimizer with a learning rate of `0.001`. The training operation is the operation in which the optimizer minimizes the loss.

Run the computational graph

To actually run the computational graph, first we initialize all of the variables in our program. The variables are the weights that are implicit in the `fully_connected` function. We run four epochs and for each epoch, we initialize our iterator object. We pass training x and training y, and then we run this loop. This loop will run as long as we have data in `next_elementelement`. So, we get the next 100 elements and then, in the next iteration, the next 100 elements, and so on. In every iteration, we run the training operation. Now, what this training operation does is ask the optimizer to adjust the parameters and the weights, a little bit in order to make better predictions.

The following screenshot shows the lines of code used for running the computational graph:

```
In [25]:  with tf.Session() as sess:
              tf.global_variables_initializer().run()
              for epoch in range(n_epochs):
                  sess.run(iterator.initializer, feed_dict={X_placeholder: X_train, y_placeholder: y_train})
                  while True:
                      try:
                          batch_data = sess.run(next_element)
                          X_batch = batch_data[0]
                          y_batch = batch_data[1]
                          sess.run(training_op, feed_dict={X: X_batch, y:y_batch})
                      except tf.errors.OutOfRangeError:
                          break
                  print("Epoch: {}".format(epoch+1))
              print("Done Trainning!")
              probabilities = probs.eval(feed_dict={X: X_test})[:,1]
```

In the end, we can get the probabilities and we can use these for evaluation purposes.

Evaluating the model with a set threshold

The `probabilities` object is produced to actually evaluate the model performance with different classification thresholds. The classification threshold can be modified for a binary classification problem and can be used for calculating the recall score, the precision, and the accuracy. On using a classification threshold of 0.16, these are the metrics that we get in the testing dataset:

```
In [26]:  y_pred = (probabilities > 0.16).astype(int)
          print('Recall: {:0.2f}'.format(100*recall_score(y_true=y_test, y_pred=y_pred)))
          print('Precision: {:0.2f}'.format(100*precision_score(y_true=y_test, y_pred=y_pred)))
          print('Accuracy: {:0.2f}'.format(100*accuracy_score(y_true=y_test, y_pred=y_pred)))

          Recall: 82.53
          Precision: 34.02
          Accuracy: 60.70
```

On calculating, we get a recall score of 82.53 percent, precision of 34.02 percent, and an accuracy of 60.7 percent.

Summary

In this chapter, we learned how to make predictions using TensorFlow. We studied the MNIST dataset and classification of models using this dataset. We came across the elements of DNN models and the process of building the DNN. Later, we progressed to study regression and classification with DNNs. We classified handwritten digits and learned more about building models in TensorFlow. This brings us to the end of this book! We learned how to use ensemble algorithms to produce accurate predictions. We applied various techniques to combine and build better models. We learned how to perform cross-validation efficiently. We also implemented various techniques to solve current issues in the domain of predictive analysis. And, the best part, we used the DNN models we built to solve classification and regression problems. This book has helped us implement various machine learning techniques to build advanced predictive models and apply them in the real world.

Other Books You May Enjoy

If you enjoyed this book, you may be interested in these other books by Packt:

Predictive Analytics with TensorFlow
Md. Rezaul Karim

ISBN: 978-1-78839-892-3

- Get a solid and theoretical understanding of linear algebra, statistics, and probability for predictive modeling
- Develop predictive models using classification, regression, and clustering algorithms
- Develop predictive models for NLP
- Learn how to use reinforcement learning for predictive analytics
- Factorization Machines for advanced recommendation systems
- Get a hands-on understanding of deep learning architectures for advanced predictive analytics
- Learn how to use deep Neural Networks for predictive analytics
- See how to use recurrent Neural Networks for predictive analytics
- Convolutional Neural Networks for emotion recognition, image classification, and sentiment analysis

scikit-learn Cookbook - Second Edition
Julian Avila, Trent Hauck, Trent Hauck, These popular $10 titles might interest you, Trent Hauck, These popular $10 titles might interest you, Learning

ISBN: 978-1-78728-638-2

- Build predictive models in minutes by using scikit-learn
- Understand the differences and relationships between Classification and Regression, two types of Supervised Learning.
- Use distance metrics to predict in Clustering, a type of Unsupervised Learning
- Find points with similar characteristics with Nearest Neighbors.
- Use automation and cross-validation to find a best model and focus on it for a data product
- Choose among the best algorithm of many or use them together in an ensemble.
- Create your own estimator with the simple syntax of sklearn
- Explore the feed-forward neural networks available in scikit-learn

Leave a review - let other readers know what you think

Please share your thoughts on this book with others by leaving a review on the site that you bought it from. If you purchased the book from Amazon, please leave us an honest review on this book's Amazon page. This is vital so that other potential readers can see and use your unbiased opinion to make purchasing decisions, we can understand what our customers think about our products, and our authors can see your feedback on the title that they have worked with Packt to create. It will only take a few minutes of your time, but is valuable to other potential customers, our authors, and Packt. Thank you!

Index

A

activation function 92
AdaBoost algorithm 11
adaptive boosting 11
artificial neural networks (ANNs)
  about 90
  multilayer perceptron 93
  perceptrons 90

B

bagging 10
bootstrap sampling 9

C

classifications, with DNN model
  about 129, 131
  architecture, defining 134
  building 132
  computational graph, running 136
  data, executing 132
  elements 131
  evaluation nodes 135
  evaluation, with set threshold 137
  Exponential Linear Unit (ELU) activation function 130
  input pipeline 133
  inputs and labels, placeholders 134
  loss function 135
  neural network, building 134
  objects for modeling, producing 133
  optimizer 135
  training operation 135
  training strategy 133
credit card dataset
  predicting 20

D

Deep Neural Networks (DNNs)
  building 122
  deep learning 96
  elements 96
  MLP model, elements 97
  regression 121
diamond dataset
  reference 12
dimensionality reduction
  and PCA 65
DNN model, TensorFlow
  architecture, defining 115
  building 115
  classification accuracy 118
  computational graph, executing 119
  data, reading 115
  elements 113
  loss function 117
  neural network, building 116
  optimizer, defining 117
  placeholders, for inputs and labels 116
  training operations 117
  training strategy 118

E

elements, MLP model
  activation function 97
  architecture 97
  loss function 98
  optimization algorithm 98
  regularization strategy 98
  training strategy 99
  weight initialization strategy 98
ensemble learning 9
ensemble methods, classification

bagging model 25
boosting model 27
credit card dataset , predicting 20
logistic regression model 24
random forest model 26
regression models 24
ensemble methods, regression
diamond dataset 12
regression models, training 15
ensemble methods
about 8
bagging 10
boosting 11
bootstrap sampling 9
random forests 11
using, for classification 20
working 9

F

feature engineering
about 72
new features, creating 72, 78
used, for improving models 80
feature importance 55
feature selection methods
about 53
dummy features with low variance, removing 54
recursive feature elimination 55, 64

H

holdout cross-validation 36
hyperparameter tuning
about 45
exhaustive grid search 46
in scikit-learn 46
tuned models, comparing with untuned models 51

I

irreducible error 87, 88

K

k-fold cross-validation
about 36

implementing 38
Leave-One-Out (LOO) cross-validation 37
models, comparing 41, 45
repeated cross-validation 37
K-Nearest Neighbors (KNN) model 15

M

Mixed National Institute of Standards and Technology (MNIST) dataset
about 112
used, for building classification model 113
multilayer perceptron (MLP) 90, 93

O

ops operation 104

P

perceptrons 90
predictive models
improving, with feature engineering 80
training 84, 86
principal component analysis (PCA)
and dimensionality reduction 65, 71
principal components 65

R

random forests 11
rectified Linear Unit (ReLU) 97
recursive feature elimination (RFE) 55
reducible errors 87, 88
regression models
bagging model 16
boosting model 17
K-Nearest Neighbors (KNN) model 15
random forests model 16
regression, with DNN model
architecture, defining 124
computational graph, executing 126
data, reading 123
elements 122
input pipeline 124
input values and labels, placeholders 124
loss function 125
model, building 125

objects for modeling 123
optimizer, defining 125
training operations 125
training strategy 123
regression
ensemble methods 11

T

TensorFlow, predictions 111
TensorFlow

about 100
computational graph 104, 110
constants 105
core concepts 103
high level 100
installation 100
low level 100
placeholders 105
session 105
tensor 104
variables 105